Voices Of Youth

Edited By Donna Samworth

First published in Great Britain in 2021 by:

Young Writers
Remus House
Coltsfoot Drive
Peterborough
PE2 9BF
Telephone: 01733 890066
Website: www.youngwriters.co.uk

All Rights Reserved
Book Design by Davina Hopping
© Copyright Contributors 2021
Softback ISBN 978-1-80015-675-3

Printed and bound in the UK by BookPrintingUK
Website: www.bookprintinguk.com
YB0488D

Foreword

Young Writers began thirty years ago. Three decades, 360 months, 1560 weeks or 10,950 days (give a leap day or two!).

To put that into context, when Young Writers first started John Major was the UK's Prime Minister, mobile phones were the size of a brick, and the World Wide Web was just a single page, not yet available to the public.

A lot has changed since then, and Young Writers has been there every step of the way, helping young poets and authors to chronicle those changes across the years through their creative writing. From the rise of technology and social media, to the fall of animal populations across the globe, to changing attitudes, we've seen it all, and young writers from across the country and across the years have explored it all through the medium of poetry.

A lot of those poets are now grown up, and may have had children of their own who are now embarking on their own creative journey, exploring the world and their feelings through words, and in the process discovering not only their skill and creativity, but also themselves. That's pretty amazing, and definitely something to celebrate!

So we decided to celebrate the only way we know how – through poetry! We asked for poems on any theme and in any style, so this birthday book is filled with eclectic poems from a range of voices. What are you waiting for? Come on in and join the Big Poetry Party.

And here's to the next 30 years!

Contents

Independent Entries

Tasmiyah Maryam	1
Simone de Almeida (14)	2
Kathryn Blades (13) & Aimee Busher (13)	8
Keziah Rigby	14
Esther Thompson (10)	17
Ellie Dinsdale (15)	18
Ella Thompson (12)	21
Ishita Ghosh	22
Catherine Dugin-Umusu (11)	25
Tasneim Badawi (11)	26
Jaylen South (13)	29
Tanisha Chowdhury (13)	30
Erica Awanife (14)	32
Iman Saihi (17)	34
Aleksandr Nikolaev (12)	37
Ivana de Almeida (11)	38
Layla Suleiman (15)	40
Courtney Rigby	42
Anisha Sahu (9)	44
Callidh Miller (14)	46
Siya Patel (13)	48
Teboho Ngwenya (15)	51
Rushaananth Srirankan (11)	52
Manha Fahad (8)	54
Melissa Pritchard (16)	56
Sofia Sonora Celma (10)	58
Anam Iftikhar (8)	60
Esma Suruliz (5)	62
Prakrith Rao (13)	64
Robert Junior Arthur (15)	66
Kashaf-Ul-Noor (18)	68
Marian Herath (17)	70
Yaana Mishra (14)	72
Kiera Thorpe (15)	74
Safiya Khalid (12)	76
Gayatri Gadepalli (10)	78
Isabelle Borg	80
Jemma Crane	82
Ashmeet Kaur (10)	84
Beatriz Suarez (15)	86
Jessica Carroll (11)	88
Isula Seneviratne (17)	90
Rebecca Sade Bashorun (7)	92
Brinna Okechukwu (13)	93
Daniel Ogundipe (12)	94
Kheevi Harcourt (13)	96
Stephanie Green (7)	98
Pranshi Gupta (12)	99
Jessica Vali-Tsang (13)	100
Vitaly Rassomakin (10)	102
Nabil Suleman (7)	104
Rachel Wilkinson (15)	105
Sally Shammaa (10)	106
Lily-Eden Bayliff (7)	108
Shiyam Thulasiraj (8)	109
Khalil Daud (13)	110
Shamaila Khan (13)	111
Maryiam Tajdin (12)	112
Izza Khan	113
Alice Watson (10)	114
Favour Adeyonu (11)	115
Alicia Cimpoeru (13)	116
Muhammad Umar Abbas (8)	117
Sophia Popova (13)	118
Aaliyah Ali	120
Alara Kunacav	122
Sidra Malik (15)	124
Mohammed-Ayaan Iftikhar (10)	125

Martha Pearson (11)	126
Cacper Dzieminski (11)	128
Ameerah Adil Salim (11)	130
Annicha Djiele (12)	131
Sukhveer Bhangu (11)	132
Karen Alexy (12)	134
Kuhu Rajadhyaksha (12)	135
Oliver Hard (16)	136
Annika Tang	138
Emmratu Blango	140
Morgan Davidson (14)	141
Dylan Watson (11)	142
Corlene Mazwi (15)	143
Rania Pannun (10)	144
Joshua Alexy (8)	146
Nona Nwajide (8)	147
Esmee Raghavan (10)	148
Hasan Suruliz (9)	149
Manreet Kaur (11)	150
Daniel Leaver (13)	151
Jaskaran Bhachu (11)	152
Mia Martin (7)	153
Prayaga Salim (10)	154
Harman Doll (14)	155
Megan Ceesay	156
Leah Bashorun (10)	157
Sophie Whitfield-Gray (12)	158
Daniella Analogbei (12)	159
Subaha Falaq Chowdhury (11)	160
Gifty-Favour Thompson (8)	161
Liela Richardson (12)	162
Darcie Wright	164
Aiza Anwaar (8)	165
Caitlyn Irving (14)	166
Shupany Sabesh (12)	167
Benjamin Doeteh (15)	168
Vari Patel (14)	169
Gilbert Phillips (8)	170
Aiza Hussain (9)	171
Maiya Ceesay	172
Alasdair James Riddell (13)	173
Aretha Tsanga	174
Ryan Watson (9)	175
Jovita Kurilenko (12)	176
Chidimma Oguledo (14)	177
Rosie Roberts-Bridgewater (13)	178
Abdullah Okelola (7)	179
Mia Gallacher (13)	180
Simisola-Zion Ajibade (11)	181
Kavish Chavda (8)	182
Ermioni Tsantikou (11)	183
Huda Ahmed (8)	184
Millie Thornton (13)	185
Zarah Khalifa (13)	186
Maheen Fahad (11)	187
Zanib Arfan (9)	188
Samaya Heywood (16)	189
Kalaya Partridge (10)	190
Eloise Fowle	191
Clayton Beaton (6)	192
Julia Hayek (10)	193
Karla Pipera (8)	194
Angel Wilkin (12)	195
Maya Dworak (10)	196
Sophia Currie (10)	197
Gurmehr Grover (14)	198
Zunairah Iqbal Raja (14)	199
Anoosha Fatima (14)	200
Matilda Rhodes (9)	201
Róise McLernon (6)	202
Ariyanna Turner-Rathbone (8)	203
Ellis Mitchell (8)	204
Callum Cayley (13)	205
Maysaa El Aoussi Hamdoun (11)	206
Austin Ford (7)	207
Katie Thompson (13)	208
Maya Judge (11)	209
Amasha Ugathri Ganeshaparan (9)	210
Jorja Cleall (10)	211
James Worth (12)	212
Vera Krauchuk-Muzhyv	213
Vadims Liss (9)	214
Erin Stedman (10)	215
Savreen Kaur (10)	216
Agastya Dainak	217

Zainab Channar (7)	218
Charlie Barton (10)	219
Alana Marie Day (12)	220
Truth Blunderfield (10)	221
Zakariya Zaidi (8)	222
Nafisa Khan (9)	223
Nasif Khan (8)	224
Simrat Kaur Gill Sandhu (10)	225
Siân Watson (7)	226
Arghojit Giri (16)	227
Amy Holding (12)	228
Emily Rudd (14)	229
Ellen Durham (8)	230
Shifa Fatima (8)	231
Elizabeth Holmes (8)	232
Leigha Mcgarva (10)	233
Briannika Rae Brown (8)	234
George Frank Gamble (7)	235
Lana Khoshnaw (6)	236
Elsa Hussain (13)	237
Archie Embleton	238
Syeda-Zahra Iftikhar (6)	239
Libbie Reid (9)	240
Nusayba Ahmed (9)	241
Gabriela Sosnowska (12)	242
Madeleine Sibley (8)	243
Logan Stewart (7)	244
Sophia Tang (7)	245
Fred Gamble (6)	246
Evia Shaw-Lewis (8)	247
Katrina Lise (6)	248
Nahida Forid (7)	249
Maham Muhammad (12)	250
Bella-May Conway (8)	251
Charlie Carroll (11)	252
Oluwasemilore Isabelle Abiola	253
Yumi Smith (8)	254

THE POEMS

I Am From...

I am from thrilling adventure books, from endless imagination and heroic quests.
I am from plates and eyeglasses, from the sparkling spotlessness, in which I see my own reflection.
I am from chocolate and ice cream, from the mouth-watering taste that melts delightfully in my mouth.

I am from scarlet-red rose bushes, from the refreshing fragrance that fills the air with a sweet aroma.
I am from the breathtakingly glorious art, from the vibrant colours, that seems to put my mind in endless creation and joy.
I am from the five prayers, from Salah and the strict rules that I follow, in the name of the Powerful Almighty Creator.

I am from suitcases and long memorable journeys, from lush green valleys to gorgeous sky blue lakes.
I am from warm-hearted parents and from annoying carefree siblings, to chaos roaming my world.
I am from ancient, heart-warming pictures, from photo albums spilling old unforgettable memories.
I am from these moments, that I will cherish forever.

Tasmiyah Maryam

Aphrodite Of The Sunrise

The morning sun has spilt through these thin, white linen curtains
And painted the blank canvas of the ceiling with a gentle, golden warmth
That - in the few blurred moments in which I stare up at it wearily -
I come to grow almost fond of.

I lie amongst crumpled sheets
And the smell of morning -
Intertwined -
With last night's mistakes,
And this morning's regret.

I turn to you,
And stroke the sleepy blush of your cheek.

Perhaps it's your hair:
Soft against my wandering lips -
Or the flowers of your perfume -

But a lonely thought traipses through my half-waking consciousness,
And for a moment,

I think I might love you -
Or want to love you at least -

And I wonder if that would be enough;

You said you loved me yesterday
And I have lived every moment since in the fear that you meant it -
We had laughed away the silence of my response -
And I thought you knew,

But your hand slipped into mine,
And I didn't have the heart to leave it.

Your eyes are fluttering open
And your face becomes a mess of pink and gold,
You look into my eyes and smile.

Are you happy I'm still here?
Happy I haven't left?
I know you expected me to
And I should have, I know -
For you are still smiling -
And something breaks in me.

Then your lips are against mine,
And I don't have the heart to pull away;

Not pulling perhaps -
But not pushing either
And as your lips work against my own in earnest,
You feel how dead they are
And move to extricate yourself from whatever this is
But, too afraid of losing the things I do not want,
I pull you against me
Closer -
Always closer -
And our lips familiarise themselves with each other
In a strange dance so foreign to me,
But which you seem to know like an old friend -

Perhaps a Ländler then -
You tried to teach me last summer
At your parents' house in Vienna
But I stepped on your toes one too many times
And you danced with that friend of yours instead.

I should have been jealous,
That was your intention I'm sure,
But the music felt nice
And the air was cold
Like the drink in my hand
And I had never felt more alive.

Our lips part
And your breathing is full of a character it usually lacks
-
That interests me;
It is as though you have forgotten you need more than me for survival,
As though you have only just remembered that
Oxygen is just as important.

Your lips are red with a passion I can only be surprised to have incited -
Your eyes blue with unshed tears -
Are they from laughter or sadness?
I know this ceiling's feelings better than I know yours;
I am not one to pass judgement
Perhaps you don't even know yourself.

But I'm looking at you
And I think this is what beauty is:
The poetry written all over your face
Which I can't quite bear to read,
Let alone touch,
For I have no right to taint something so divine.

My mother once told me,
That to sin against beauty is to sin against God himself
-

I suppose I am the greatest of all sinners then
And God must hate me.

When I go to Hell,
Will you love me still?

In my internal meanderings I appear to have lost myself
And you've since slipped from the ocean of sheets
And, like Aphrodite emerging from the foam,
You descend upon my mortal being,
And lay your head upon my chest

I don't have the heart to push you off.

And as your breathing returns to its usual, mindless monotony
My mind is silent for a while,
And all at once, my life is reduced to three simple statements:

You love me
And I want to love you
That's enough.

"Don't leave," you mumble,
Your trembling, sleep-worn voice settling like dew upon my chest

And I don't.

Simone de Almeida (14)

The Tale Of Sun And Moon

This is the tale of Sun and Moon,
One that has rarely been heard,
Some say it's fictional, some say it's true,
It may be a story that never occurred.

Whether this tale is true or not,
I shall tell it to you today,
With your biscuits and your chamomile tea,
Sit down and hear what I have to say.

Sun and Moon were just two lonely people,
In their worlds, which were full of hate,
One day they would finally meet,
Their love would seal their fate.

The two were quite like yin and yang,
He was quiet and she was loud,
Opposites that work very well,
But their love was not allowed.

Sun and Moon were perfect soulmates,
Their love no one could comprehend,
They thought their love could last forever,
But they came to a nasty end.

Their worlds were parallel to each other,
But they never could agree,
Each one thought they were superior,
So war was declared, no one was free.

Moon was the princess, always rebelling,
Not listening to a word that was said,
Her parents were always very worried,
Of what would become of this feisty redhead.

Sun was the child of a businessman,
Who had discovered something great,
A portal that led to a parallel world,
One that they grew to hate.

In Moon's world, the portal was seen as a curse,
They tried desperately to take it away,
It failed every time because Sun's world had found,
A way to get it to stay.

This story started in Moon's grand palace,
Where she heard of a worrying tale,
The guards were trying to close up a portal,
But each attempt so far was a fail.

Being a princess, 16 years of age,
Curiosity dictated her life,
She was branded a rebel because of this trait,
Her parents doubted she'd ever be a wife.

Since she knew of the portals between the two worlds,
Naturally she had to know more,
She waited until each of the guards were gone,
Then crept around the palace, floor after floor.

After minutes she arrived at the palace entrance,
Casting shadows were looming and dark,
With some food in her bag and her jumper wrapped tight,
She stepped into her garden, as big as a park.

She'd only been looking for 20 minutes or so,
Before a rustling came from a tree,
A light suddenly shone, taking her by surprise,
Blinding her so she couldn't see.

Possibilities flooded her mind like a wave,
She was scared but she wouldn't back down,
She peered around the tree but tripped and she fell,
Landing on the ground with a frown.

Looking down to see the problem,
She found that her feet were stuck,

The light had appeared, it was right in front,
It seemed to be sucking her out of the muck.

Her screams were echoed across the park,
As she rose up in the sky,
And now surrounded by a whirlwind of colours,
She felt as though she could fly.

She didn't feel like that for long though,
As she tumbled to the floor,
It only occurred to her that she had found the portal,
When she saw a figure standing at the door.

She braced herself for the figure coming over,
Her hands curled up into fists,
The figure put their hands in a surrendering pose,
So she grudgingly lowered her wrists.

The figure was a man, about the same age as her,
He was small and his hair was dark,
Moon's heart started pounding, his face was so sweet,
He lit up the room, bare and stark.

"Hello," said the man. "My name is Sun."
"What's yours?" he asked with a grin,
"M-Moon," said the girl, suppressing a smile,
She was mesmerised by the glow of his skin.

"So where do you come from?" Sun then asked the girl,
She replied, "I think you know."
"I was about to head into the portal," he said,
"But obviously I was too slow."

"Yes, you were," Moon said with a smile,
"Do you believe in love at first sight?"
"Yes," said the boy, coming close to her,
And they kissed with all their might.

"I love you," he said as they drew apart,
"I love you too," she replied,
Then the guards rushed in, weapons at the ready,
And *bang*... Moon had died.

"No!" screamed Sun as he kicked down the guards,
Stealing a gun for himself,
He pointed it to his heart and suddenly declared,
"I will never leave her by herself!"

He fell to the ground, perfectly in line,
With his lover by his side,
The perfect soulmates, together at peace,
In Heaven together they did glide.

So as you can see, this tale is grim,
Not the nicest one you will hear,

But Sun and Moon live happily together,
So you will never have to fear.

So goodnight to you, my dearest friend,
Sleep tight and rest in your bed,
And one final thing before I go,
Remember what I said.

Kathryn Blades (13) & Aimee Busher (13)

The Bottom-Pecking Bird

This might sound crazy or even absurd,
But have you ever heard of the bottom-pecking bird?

You might say it's unreal or even not true,
But has this strange encounter ever happened to you?

So let me enlighten you, it might make more sense,
About the strange event that happened over the fence.

It happened one Saturday at a quarter past three,
When my neighbour shouted out aloud, "Oh goodness, gracious me."

With a shout and a squeal and a squawking, "What the heck?"
My neighbour became a victim of the bird's nasty peck.

There was a flash of red and green, followed by purple and blue,
Leaving Miss Jones asking, "Child, was that you?"
"No," said I, "it was not me,
But that nasty, vicious bird right there, hiding in that tree."

I peeped through the branches at two beady eyes,
Which made me jump backwards, (that took me by surprise.)

The last thing I expected was to see such a sight,
Seeing that creature gave me such a fright.

For there I spied a bird, without a care in the world,
Its wings of perfect colour, elegantly unfurled.
I looked deep into his eyes... black as blackest coal,
I could tell he was naughty, his eyes an entrance to his soul.

I waited and watched, not sure what I would see,
And the bird stuck again right in front of me.

He moved down my street, with not a walk but a trot,
And proceeded to peck old Moaning Maggie's very large bot'.

The gardener, who was weeding at house number 4,
Was next to be pecked, falling flat on the floor.

"Oi you rascal," said the gardener, jumping to his feet,
Then he yelled a rude word that I simply can't repeat.

The lollipop lady keeping the roads safe and clear,
Was next to be pecked on her traffic-stopping rear.

"Ohhhh you naughty, naughty bird," she shouted, attempting a kick,
Then she joined in the chase waving her lollipop stick.

It was hard not to laugh as the bird pecked its prey,
The postman, the milkman were also pecked that day.

The bird ran through the town pecking bottoms that he saw.
Then the police took action, shouting, "That's against the law!"

Unaware of the chase the bird plodded on,
Then turned and pecked the chief constable right on the bum!
"You're under arrest!" the chief constable exclaimed,
Fitting the pesky bird with cuffs and chains.

But with one mighty peck, the chain was chopped in two,
Then up, up and away the bird he quickly flew.

So please be on your guard, next time you're at the beach, park or fair...
This bird's next mission might be your derriere!

Yes, I know, this sounds crazy, even a tad absurd,
But now you know the story of the bottom-pecking bird.

Keziah Rigby

Our Earth

Earth and great lands stretching endlessly
I dream to travel to the lost city of the Congo
and to see whales passing down a coast where no one lives
while dancing with the sea waves
as the rhythm of the water sets my soul free.

The strong winds brewing as the rain drops down and drifts into the sea
destroying everything in his path
reducing magnificent buildings to rubble
while bringing coolness to the warm parts of the world.
In the cool, peaceful Alaska, silence is broken as the powerful wind bursts in
causing animals fighting with their own siblings for warm shelter
While at the other side of the earth,
the sun blasting its dangerous UV rays towards the earth
burning as people start begging for some cold rain,
While the Alaskan people are freezing to death
wishing for warmth and as they get warmth, everything is green.
Everything is peaceful now around the world.
What sunshine is to flowers and smiles are to humanity.

Esther Thompson (10)

The Lighthouse Keeper

A clammy palm flush against a pane,
The glass a source of great disdain,
The destructive scene - a swirling mass,
Terrifyingly vivid through the grimy glass,
For not a single vessel would survive,
A storm to leave not one alive.

The rotted pane streaked with mould,
Did little to hide the scene unfold,
Fingers knotted and shakily placed,
Did wring themselves to stop their shake,
For not a single vessel would survive,
A storm to leave not one alive.

A matted beard the colour of ocean spray,
Did rest upon a doublet of dirtied grey,
A fisherman's spirit encased his soul,
A source of comfort for a man so old,
For not a single vessel would survive,
A storm to leave not one alive.

The tumultuous waves enveloped and consumed,
Driving the landscape to an inescapable doom,
The lighthouse keeper looked on with woe,

Alone on the island, he allowed his fear to show,
For not a single vessel would survive,
A storm to leave not one alive.

The lighthouses' stubborn facade,
Melted under the menacing gaze,
Of a storm so fierce the island shook,
The lighthouse keeper could scarcely look,
For not a single vessel would survive,
A storm to leave not one alive.

Poseidon sent another platoon,
Of soldiers cloaked in robes of doom,
Bedecked with shells as sharp as blades,
To send defenders to early graves,
For not a single vessel would survive,
A storm to leave not one alive.

The infamous waves cruel and malicious,
Savaged the landscape with intentions so vicious,
Streams of heavenly light fell from inky skies,
Breaking the darkness and stifling battle cries,
For not a single vessel would survive,
A storm to leave not one alive.

A scruffy dog of gentle temper,
Comforted by the heat of a dying ember,

Nuzzled a wet snout into his master's knee,
Who smiled in spite of his fear running free,
For not a single vessel would survive,
A storm to leave not one alive.

And so, the keeper closed his eyes,
Listening to the war outside,
His fear abated for a while,
Certain he would survive this trial,
The storm would surely pass in time,
And though the stench of death and crime,
Would linger in the salty air,
Sailors' lives stolen without a care,
Peace to those who died tonight,
Missing the lighthouse's saving light,
The shriek of winds suddenly stilled,
The old keeper's heart was promptly filled,
With a resignation too potent to dilute,
A realisation that wouldn't mute,
For not a single vessel would survive,
A storm to leave not one alive.

Ellie Dinsdale (15)

Seasons

As frost falls from the crystal-blue sky,
Snow simply arrives within the blink of an eye.
The graceful snow is pearly white,
And it gets colder and colder throughout the night.
As the snow slowly starts to melt,
It finally gets warmer than you've ever felt.
Then the trees start to bloom now it's spring,
Then life comes back to everything.
The grass is greener than it ever could be,
Spring is here! Everyone is smiling with glee.
All of a sudden it gets hotter and hotter here,
This is going to be the hottest in the year.
Finally, we go into the luxurious pool,
Which makes us happy, nice and cool.
Now we go down to the beach and relax,
Which takes my happiness to the max.
Why are the hot days going away?
Oh, I really wish they would stay.
Now the leaves are falling,
This is very shocking.
Everything starts to change and then!
The four seasons are starting all over again.

Ella Thompson (12)

The Tragedy Called 'Our World'

Passionate, articulate, magnificent and ludicrous,
What our politicians are described as,
But is that really serious,
Cos it must be a joke,
What else could it be?
I'd describe it as corruption, ostentation and greed.
That is what plays us behind the scenes.

You call this a democracy?
When everyone's pitted against their own brothers,
People are enslaved by mind,
And are hypnotised to kill others.
You call this a democracy?
I think not,
When those who created a democracy,
Take away all we've got.
Our freedom,
Our choice,
Our incessant flow of words,
Our kingdom,
Our voice,
And our money and clothes.

I call this fake jurisdiction, prying and unfair,
We steal people's information,
And then judge them for it because of their race, sexuality or lack of education,
When all they need is a chance and a break from discrimination.

When violence is used to solve an uncomfortable situation,
We know that our politicians lie with themselves and not their nation.
When people stop ruling over others,
with blackmail, stress, and spite,
Then only our youth can earn a new life.
You say that we're good and kind and nice,
But what do you say? When our nation is flooded with bloody knives.
Have you helped that at all, have you helped our health,
All you do is sit behind a wall of your wealth.
Why aren't the people who need to be saved?
Is it because of a lack of police force
Or another name,
Who bribes and kills and hides from fame,
And hurts children and averts the blame.

What about the brainwashed ones?
Their lives would come to a worth,
If only they weren't forced to dedicate their lives to reduce flesh to bones.
What about kidnapping, trafficking, drugs and killing,
If only the politicians were involved with this,
But not literally of course,
As it already is.

The brain should be a wonder of the world,
Since not many can understand it,
But exploit it to no good.
If only more people understood,
An individual's fight,
And politicians could put more work into what is wrong and what is right.
If only our presidential campaigns were less pretentious to votes,
And an actual person stood up,
Who knows the price of self-worth?
As this is getting to be long,
I hope you've found the issues within our earth,
All I've mentioned are the people and crime,
But don't worry there's much worse.

Ishita Ghosh

The Three Lockdowns

The three lockdowns were something for me
Sometimes I was upset, sometimes I was happy.
But it seems as though it was all okay
Because I worked through it up to this day.

In the first lockdown we got stuck with family friends
And for some reason, it felt like it would never end.
It was like an endless lifetime just repeating:
Schoolwork, eating, speaking, sleeping.

Before the second lockdown I finally got to say hi
But then I suddenly realised how much work I'd missed in Yr 5.
Then when it finally came,
There was nothing, it felt like an empty video game.

During the third lockdown we finally moved
And I was suddenly an expert at homeschool.
Although it sounds great, it wasn't really
We had gone through a lot of moving and it wasn't easy.

This is my journey through the three lockdowns.
All I have to say to COVID-19 is look at me now!

Catherine Dugin-Umusu (11)

The Seasons

I wake up to a cold shiver
I wrap up in my favourite blanket and put my cosy slippers on
Smelling some warm hot chocolate with soft marshmallows all ready for me
As soon as I drink all my hot chocolate
I get my wellies on, gloves and hat
As well as my coat, can't forget that
I run outside to the cold shining snow and start building my snowman
It has some old buttons as eyes, stones as a mouth,
And of course, a carrot as the nose

After a while, I come back in as the day is ending
I get my pyjamas on and read a book
Soon, I am fast asleep...

Three months later...

I wake up as hot as I've ever been
I am tried but also in a good mood
I look outside the bathroom window and to my surprise, it's raining
The weather is just confusing!

Since the weather isn't very nice
I decide to watch a movie
I need some snacks to eat during the movie
So I go to the shops and buy some snacks and drinks
The movie starts and it is great fun
But it is coming to an end
Unfortunately, I didn't finish the movie
I sleep halfway through
I mostly do that

Three months later...

I have set up a fan since the weather is really hot
Seems like it worked very well
Since it is a lovely day me and my friend decide we need to have a day off and relax
I have gotten my shades on and some sandals and I am off to the beach
I meet my friend there and we go for a swim in our blue swimming costumes
We are both hungry and agree to eat at a restaurant
We prefer to eat dessert first as it is our choice

We both decide to have a fun sleepover but as soon as I get to my friend's house
I fall asleep since I am exhausted!

Three months later...

I wake up and look outside my bathroom window
Orange, yellow and red is all I can see.
Trees covered in autumn leaves waving around
I get dressed and eat my breakfast
I decide to go for a little walk for some fresh air
I step in the colourful leaves and make crunchy noises with my feet
I make a leaf angel and later sit by the trees, watching leaves fall down
I have so much fun.

Tasneim Badawi (11)

Take That Autism!

I used to be different because of my needs,
it wasn't my friend it was my enemy!
I used to be dysfunctional and used to cry
because I couldn't make any friends and I didn't know why.
I used to ask my mum if I could ever have a brother,
but at that time I didn't even live with my mother.

As I got older I would go to the court,
there was a plethora of people all talking to each other.
I wish back then I could have made some friends
because I'm turning 13 and only have five friends.

My nan and my uncle, they have stuck by my side
they have helped me get through some really tough times.
Now I can talk and talk I shall.
No one or nothing can put me down.
I have nearly overcome my autism.

Now I'm not stuck in this solitary prison,
I've got friends beside me and I am really, really grateful.
Now I know what to say and I know what to do,
I'm the first to introduce when I meet someone new.

Jaylen South (13)

It's Strange, Don't You Think?

It's strange, don't you think?
The way you make my heart sink,
to depths greater than I'm familiar with.
Sometimes I wonder, could you be a myth?
A myth coming to haunt me,
to cloud my thoughts and blind me.
Though I cannot fault you any further,
as it was thanks to you, I was finally able to see.
To truly see, the colour and beauty of myself.
And as the days continue to pass,
the butterflies which once overtook my stomach when
our eyes had locked have flown away.
I always knew they would never last,
yet it was as if my heart was in need of a cast.
Still, an unfamiliar feeling it really was.
Nevertheless, the days advanced
and surely enough we repeatedly locked eyes,
just as easily as you said your byes.
However, this time was certainly not the same as the last.
This time, I was no longer greeted with a perfect face,
how could this possibly be the case?

In fact, I was faced with nothing but countless flaws,
one after the other.
Flaws that I had never noticed before.
Perhaps that was the curse of love,
to be blinded by your heart so much as to willingly
reject the imperfections of the person you want so
badly to be perfect.

Tanisha Chowdhury (13)

Soul Searching

I'm back here; somewhere I always end up and even though my head knows better; my heart won't let go
The cold breeze is flowing right through me
And I just can't stop thinking about who I used to be
I should probably shut out these feelings like I usually do
But every time I close my eyes I picture you
It's too late for regrets I know
But I wonder time and time again if there was another way
I know you're living the best life you could possibly
But is it wrong that I'd rather have you right here close to me
The sound of your heartbeat is all that I have left
My imagination soaring, I'm smiling, thinking about what could have been
I could have held you close one last time
But instead I let you go
In losing you I think I lost me
You'll never see that you were more than just a part of me
My heart's locked, hidden, already buried deep
it's a secret vault and only you hold the key
It takes every last bit of my strength to move on and bury the past like everyone excepts me to

But underneath it all I'm still trembling at the thought of seeing you
This was more than just a simple mistake
It was a decision that little did I know would forever burden me
And maybe I should close my eyes and shut it all out
Maybe I'm holding on to something I can never have
Maybe I should stop dreaming and live in the present, not my fading memories
But I'd give anything to just be able to feel again
I'm still out here wondering where in the world you are
If every day that goes by is another chance that you get to be happy
I wouldn't change that for the world even if it's without me
Through every breath I take destroys every part of me right down to my core
And longing for you creates an excruciating pain in my chest
When I take my last breath
I'll find comfort in the fact that you were the best mistake that I'll never regret.

Erica Awanife (14)

Best I Love

Best I love, the season of Ophelia
The gallop of new life amidst hills of green
Out peeks her head, fair maiden of spring
Herald of primroses, tulips, and violets alike
Quaint and cosy cottages doused in daffodils
The cherry tree blushes shades of grace
Somewhere a siren sings a sunken song
Down by Old Malden's riverbank
Her Garland, painted by springtide's kiss
Ophelia, pre-Raphaelite beauty
Now a poppy.

Best I love, the season of Icarus
Wax wings that taint the summer air
In sonnets of old, and songs of praise
Adam's ale turns to a calm morning dew
Swifts and swallows perched in bliss
An amorous look - lovers in fair Verona
Plum-coloured foxgloves
Hiding a midsummer melody
In the bosom of a deer, listen close
The soft beating of wings slows...
The sun has set

And in a eulogy of morning birds
Icarus, gone.

Best I love, the season of Catherine
Gossamer strung by a careful creature
Crimson fingers of the autumn crocus
A harvest filled with forage and fruits
On still November eves, robins nestle close
The copper leaves shed away
Bare-rooted alder and aspen trees stand,
Watching the lady of Thrushcross grange
Who lived her life, unaware of the fire
That copper-red flame
Etched into the hues of jealous eyes
Alas! Buried is she, overlooking the moors
That she ever so loved.

And in the cold earth,
Lay Ophelia, Icarus, and Catherine.
Enshrined with winter's gentle caress
Hues of frost-laden snow
Bathe the streets as songbirds hum
Soft is the silence, barren is the land
A stag lifts its head, inhales the chilly air
Berries and snowdrops

Pansies and parsnips
Best I love, the season where all comes to an end.

Iman Saihi (17)

A World Of Wonders

The wonders of the world, the mythical creatures,
The wonderful river, the towering trees;
Everything in this land is glorious - but there's one thing:
The sword that intrigues, yet keeps everyone safe.

It is sealed shut in the temple of light
Where only the person in possession of a heroic heart
Will be able to claim the sword when the evil arrives
The only one that can destroy the malice of evil at the blink of an eye.

But the sword has turned into a legend,
The last time it was unsheathed was over ten thousand years ago
And it has rested in the temple since then, waiting for its next use,
Which is bound to happen soon.

The sword itself is rusting,
Waiting for the day of its rebirth -
Waiting for the hero to come and rescue,
So it can rise like a phoenix
And save the world.

Aleksandr Nikolaev (12)

Making A Masterpiece

When my paintbrush hits the paper, a new adventure is unlocked
A chance to dive into the ocean of my imagination
A chance to mould a masterpiece from nothing but a mere splodge of clay
So in I go
Into a land of wonders
To the desert of possibilities and the jungle of creativity.
With a pencil in hand, I feel motivated and adventurous.
So if you think I'm going to draw a simple little flower, you aren't even close.

Maybe I'll create a landscape that stretches across the page
Capturing a beautiful moment with a few strokes of paint
Making a gradient of dark to light
To showcase the beauty of day and night

But dark colours can be too realistic and bleak
I'll go and give myself a bit of freedom
Add a dash of red here and a blob of green there
And I'll soar like a bird in my vibrant, wild world

Doubts try to cloud my visions
What if things go wrong, I keep on thinking
Maybe I should just start another drawing
And though I think about those thoughts, I have to keep on going

Relaxed, pleased, accomplished and relieved
That's how I feel after creating a masterpiece
And when I spend so much time on every little bit
Everything fits together like a jigsaw and I really love it

I don't want to paint something that people have painted 1,000 times before
I want to create something that will make people think and imagine
And even though it won't always turn out great
I hope it will bring a smile to at least one person's face.

Ivana de Almeida (11)

Pretty When She Cries...

She bites her lip hard enough,
It's bound to bleed.
She inhales deep enough
Like it's her last breath.
She blinks slow enough,
Disappointment in her gaze.

At 11pm, when everyone's asleep, the tears began.
Today's different, it begins at 3am.
The knot in her stomach tightens,
The lump in her throat forms.
She wakes, runs to the bathroom,
Locks the door, turns on the tap.

Apparent sleepless nights drag under her eyes,
Pulling her face down, down, down.
Crying is a waste of time, yet here she is again.
It is a pathetic excuse to feel sorry for herself.
Believing it'll drown her problems
Only to find she is gasping for air.

She cries stony rivers 'til all 42 muscles are numb,
'Til she tires enough she is assured blissful sleep.
She was taught that crying showed feeling.
Why's there no feel behind her tears?

Mascara from the day before
Smears her rosy cheeks.

Her lids heavy,
With barren eyes an unrecognisable corpse looks at her.
She dares a glance into its stare,
Watching how, day by day, it loses its brightness.
Stripping the hollow haze of pallid light away,
Relinquishing to obscure darkness -
Into an endless void of obsidian.

She bites her lip hard enough,
Metallic warmth seeps through her mouth.
She exhales sharp enough,
Present with a bland salt hanging thick in the air.
She blinks long enough,
Now guaranteed a night of undisturbed sleep.

She turns the tap off,
Unlocks the door and walks to her room.
She slides under her covers,
Feeling calmer yet drained.
But relief is present in her gentle breaths.
Because she knows, she only feels pretty when she cries.

Layla Suleiman (15)

Pride

People who are a part of LGBTQ+ should have pride.
Instead they have cried, suffered thoughts of suicide and to some extents even died.
Worldwide, a series of homicides has been committed to people who identified as something as simplified as bi.
There is a great divide as society did decide that people of pride were an outside.
With the constant abuse of children, its leads people to hide,
Not confide because they know they would be denied as they identified as pride.
Children are scared to come out to their parents 'cause they feel they would be mortified,
Terrified instead of being satisfied for who their child is.
Thankfully, as society grows we understand that we need to be allied,
dedicate a month so those of pride can be glorified,
so we can feel qualified to live on the inside.
Not on the outside.
But I am certified that people still provide hate crimes.
They abide by rules that they were supplied that specified, those of pride were wrong.
It makes me think, who gave them the authority, to spread such dishonesty, inequality so audibly.

Calling those of pride an irregularity, searching them with harsh peculiarity making us feel like an obscurity.
Those people feel as if they have a priority and think it's okay to shame someone's sexuality
and uses the wrong terminology to make us feel like a comedy.
It's shameful, horribly and terribly shameful.
We all need security, there is no priority.
We should all live our lives in equality and responsibly.

Courtney Rigby

The Seasons

Spring

The flowers bloom and there's a gentle, warm breeze...
And there are lovely blossoms in swaying trees.
Moving by the wind, the trees harmonisingly dance
Looking at them will put you in a trance.
The lambs play in fields and the rabbits jump along
The birds tweet to each other, singing a sweet song.

Summer

The kids see the sun shining and smell the barbecue!
Summer, they get out of bed and shout, "Whooo!"
They find their dog in sunglasses and on a floaty!
Their parents are barbecuing roast chicken!
Before they jump in the pool they feel their heart quicken.
They're hitting the beach - finally, fetch the beach ball.
They go through the roads and finally reach there, finding a lighthouse, so proud and tall.

Autumn

Put on your woolly hats and get your coats, please!
Nobody wants to go outside and freeze!
Red, orange and yellow leaves fall down from the trees.

The squirrels wake up to find acorns raining down!
They sorted them into colour piles: red, orange, yellow and... finally brown!
Stampede! They charge into their piles of leaves.
Oh - he scared me - the dog was in hiding in the red pile!

Winter

The polar bears wake up and roll snowballs.
The kids wake up to see that the snow falls.
They get their earmuffs, hats and coats.
They roll up different-sized snowballs
They steal a carrot and a bag of chocolate buttons - guess what they're making?
The thought of the snow stopping would be heartbreaking!
Sneak attack! Snowballs fly in opposite directions!

Anisha Sahu (9)

In This World

In this world in our day and age,
True love I have never believed in as it is so hard to gauge,
We are told in storybooks and fairy tales,
From when we were little, we thought love never failed,
We grew up to believe the world we live in is amazing,
When you grow up though every day is phasing,
The wars, the attack, the hate,
But we are taught to care more about our weight,
Society pushes us to care more about our looks,
Going through the thick glossy pages of magazine books,
We sit and stare into space,
Thinking about how easily we could be replaced,
We know there is always going to be someone prettier and smarter,
We think we always and only get used as a head starter,
As women and girls we are taught to be scared of men,
That we should walk in groups and be home by ten,
If we come away from protecting our girls and focus on teaching our boys,
That it's okay to cry and show emotion and play with dolls and Barbie toys,

We all know that's it's not all men,
They're ones that are gentle and kind and the problem is not them,
These kind sweet boys we all know will grow into the men we can trust,
It's when these boys are surrounded by toxic masculinity and bad stereotypes that are unjust,
Society raises and bullies the boys into the men we fear,
They think that it doesn't make them manly if they shed a tear,
Girls are taught to be there for girls and boys are taught to fight boys,
We shouldn't put social pressure on our kids,
But we sit there and let it happen and no one makes one little noise.

Callidh Miller (14)

Life Goes On

The world drifts to sleep,
Bed in a glistening white blanket,
Darkness pours in,
Days end before they have started.
Silence.
All life is buried deep,
After a long, troubling year.

Yet soon the first drops fall,
As the heavens share with us their tears,
We hear their cry,
We feel their call.
Before long,
The first flowers bloom,
Bursting with colour,
As Mother Nature breaks free from her cocoon.

All of a sudden,
The lights grow brighter,
Day by day,
Oranges, yellows and pinks,
Invade the sky,
While the impatient youth come out to play.
The grass becomes alive with creatures,
An endless cacophony of sounds,

This strong spell appears unbreakable,
As if a whole new world has been found.

Yet as quickly as this spark is ignited,
The winds blow it away,
Acorns and chestnuts litter the ground,
The jewels of each autumnal day.
Yet each moment,
Each second,
Still brings with it,
Colour.
Adventure.
Hope.
Hope of a new beginning.
Hope for what comes next.

And so the Earth continues on,
Swiftly sliding from one season,
To another.
Each one hosting its own unique,
Magic.
Winter suffers alongside us,
Spring hopes for us,
Summer smiles at us,
Autumn explores with us.

They say nothing lasts forever,
So those cruel times where we suffer,
Where we cry,
Where we fall,
Will pass through,
In the end,
Making us stronger.
For though darkness often creeps in,
It is up to us to find the light.
To give, not to want.
To smile, not to cry.
To celebrate, not to forget.
Because in all its sorrows,
Its pains,
Its tears,
Life goes on.

Siya Patel (13)

A Blink & Breath

Beatrice taunted by Benedick 'my dear Lady Disdain!'

Autonomously the gears in my body shift
Fuelled three times a day, accompanied by eight glasses of mineral's greatest gift
A continuous spectrum of thoughts lie adrift
Back and forth the synapses go, hoping for some sense of artificial lift

Feelings, emotions, desires all too much the same
Headphones plugged in, someone is calling my name
My body aches for the eight hours it deserves, however, my heart and lungs put the rest to shame
Tonight, a warm blanket and dim light are in the frame

Dreading a woeful sorrow
My engine cries for the clockwork of tomorrow
Right now I ask myself the rhetorical question: can time be borrowed?
For its ambitions is no longer hollow

Knowledge is a pathway of love's greatest pains
Through perception is all that remains
'Till death do us part' which sustains
When tomorrow comes we shall rightfully reign.

Teboho Ngwenya (15)

The Sea's Moods

The sea is in the sort of mood,
For wrecking, ravaging, destroying
The cruel dark ocean needs its food
With helpless sailors it is toying

Once proud ships torn to pieces
Masts rotting at the bottom of the sea
It's rotting as rage and danger the sea releases
Filling the world with debris

Great horses through the ocean roaming
Galloping freely of their own will
Striding gallantly, manes a-foaming
The wave rides on, not staying still

Round and round goes the ride of death
Coming here, going there
Almost like the ocean's breath
The great whirlpool you must beware

Oh wait, the sea's changing its mood
It no longer seeks food
The great depths are now fully fed
There is no longer reason to dread

The grand blue sea, a resplendent sight
I could stare at it all night
The calm winds blow the sea at my feet
This sight has made my day complete

The golden sand buried beneath
The kelp around stones making a wreath
The sea so calm and peaceful
It makes me feel so cheerful.

Undersea creatures can now be seen
Strands of seaweed look like string beans
The sun makes the sea a carpet of diamonds
To everyone relaxing on the glorious islands

The sun collapsing into different colours
Exploding right on the sea
Pink, orange, yellow and red
It is a beautiful sight to be seen.

Rushaananth Srirankan (11)

Banana Bread

Silky, smooth, white flour-like glistening sand in the desert,
Mixed with the brown sugar, grainy like some dirt.

Soft, powdery mixture rustling slowly in a bowl,
Take a fragile egg and poke it to make a hole.

Tap! Pop! Crackle!
Time to be alert and tackle!!

Eggs have a hard shell but inside is slipperiness,
Ripe and sweet bananas turn into a slimy mess.

Mixing eggs and bananas makes a sound very squishy,
I hope I am doing it right and my recipe is not fishy.

A wet and slippery mixture looking like an ocean of slime,
My tummy is rumbling for a snack, I know it is the time.

Wrinkled crunchy walnuts crushed in my hands,
Sweet and luscious chocolate chips look like they got suntanned.

Cut the baking paper in a shape that is not round,
Fixing the paper inside the tin makes a loud scrunching sound.

Incy wincy chocolate chips resemble my freckled doll Betsy,
Tiny toppings spread all around like a million stars in a galaxy.
Turn the oven up high and wait for it to ding,
Slowly and gently the mixture rises like a spring.

Thirty minutes later, the oven starts beeping loudly,
Waiting for my family to taste my bread proudly.

Wrinkly, bumpy crust looks like an old man's skin,
Delicious and scrumptious crumbs scattered all over my chin.

Slice of banana bread is like a fluffy pancake,
Melting in my mouth, making my taste buds shake.

Moist cake with crunchy nuts and oozing chocolate in every bite,
Mouth-watering banana bread is perfect for wintery nights!

Manha Fahad (8)

Mother And Daughter

Eyes filled with forever love
You take care of me and for that I'm eternally grateful.
A vow, to be the best person
I can be
You idolised me to become kinder and bravest.

A mother and daughter, a relationship unlike no other
Makes me feel special to have a mother like you
And yet, you've taught me that I can do the impossible.
Your guidance and generosity always impresses me so
I aspire to be an amazing role model
Just like you are every day
Our bond grows stronger and deeper.

Fate brought us together, but your love spiked a part that makes me who I am
And this creates a beautiful picture in my mind when I think of you.
Faith and hope, I appreciate everything you do for me
And I'll always be here.

A mother and daughter, a connection that can be felt within minutes
It melts my heart as I know I have you forever.
When a tough situation occurs I remember the advice you've given

It helps me take on challenges with ease, motivation and determination.
You're in my heart and on my mind
No matter what I do with myself.

Experiencing the world, you'll pick me up
And when I'm down you show me how to get back up again after being afraid.
You're my rock and shield from the outside world
Where things may get dangerous.

Melissa Pritchard (16)

The Long Caribbean Vacation

In the middle of cold, cold February,
That was when my dad told me, "How about we have a getaway vacation?"
It sounded crazy!
But we booked our tickets and flew to the breathtaking Dominican Republic.
We stayed in a hotel with a pool, but then we realised we were quite a fool.
Why stay in four walls, when we could actually experience the Island?
So we bought a car and drove around,
We drove for a month until we found a lovely village.
We looked quite different, so there were some stares,
But soon we had many friends.
We found a river where we swam and snorkelled, to the point where I was like a champion swimmer!
We found an apartment that suited our needs,
Then we bought a motorcycle just like all the locals do.
Over time we found astonishing places, even a waterfall with pressure stronger than a wall!
All this has been very fun!
Travelling, living with fewer amenities and mosquitos, but you can't stay on vacation forever.

We left in July, which is why I say;
I miss you Rosi, with your loving heart and loyalty,
I miss you Rahianny, with our adventures and fun,
I miss you Mama Julia's family, where we were welcome at any time.
Oh I miss your scorching sun, coconuts, habichuelas, rivers, landscape and mangos,
The beautiful Caribbean island.

Sofia Sonora Celma (10)

The Candle That Never Got Put Out

On the Eiffel Tower there was a luxurious parade,
Some sedentary individuals were even starting a trade.
Sitting lonely on the circular table, leaning on a mahogany flowerpot, was a singular candle,
Slurping some acrid cooking oil and observing the people at a curious angle.
"When am I going to be blown out?" the candle lamented to itself.
"This is so silly, people are even dressed as elves."
A couple of folks were blissfully playing minigolf,
As a various amount of children were pretending to be Rudolph.
The candle, now licking desiccated coconuts of a macaroon,
Was trying his best not to roast the balloons.
Dogs were yawning, like a lion opening its mouth in the savannah,
Some kids were joyously drawing a piranha.
"Someone, just please blow me out,
I need to do other things, such as watching a plant sprout.
I can't stay stuck here like a fig stuck on a tree,
I need to be free, like a roaming monkey.

The wind is whistling and the trees are giving a loud groan,
But still, I just won't be blown."
Maids were cooking, like a valorous knight,
Cooking the best prawns with all their might.
"If I don't get put out, I will be confiscated,
I feel like the bees, being so busy, missing out on the fun and just suddenly pass out.
I'm a candle, not a chair,
And I'm definitely not the candle's heir."

Anam Iftikhar (8)

Mr Pig

Mr Pig went inland
He went to the seaside, he went to the beach
And he went to the farm and he went to the cave
He went into the shark's mouth, he went into the shark's tummy
He wandered away and explored as well
He swam in a ring by the water in the shark's tummy
And Mr Pig found his own home in the shark's tummy
And guess where it was?
In a water bottle in the shark's tummy
I wonder why oh, oh, oh
That's very strange, that's so strange
Why ever is a pig going in a shark's tummy
And that's strange because Mr Pig met Esma in the shark's tummy
And then the shark swam, swam, swam
Until the shark saw Mummy Pig
Mummy Pig said, "Where's Mr Pig?
I will go shopping without Mr Pig because Mr Pig said he was going to wander away somewhere!"
So Mummy Pig did go shopping
And then Mummy Pig got lots of pig clothes which were pink
And then Mummy Pig bought a lovely T-shirt for Mr Pig

And then Mummy Pig bought a lovely statue of Mr Pig
And then Mr Pig was in the shark's tummy
He cut one of the shark's teeth
And then the shark had a toothache
And then Mr Pig escaped from the shark
And went with Esma
And Mummy Pig was so happy that she had a new friend called Esma.

Esma Suruliz (5)

The Day They're Remembered

The war, the calamity that once occurred,
The lives of ordinary soldiers not once been heard.
The people who fought for their country now believed,
A war was over, and they were all relieved.

75 years since this awful tragedy took place
And everyone wanted it to finish with haste.
The loved ones' souls to heaven they will now go,
As they fought against the evil fascist foe.

Heroes returned from war shattered and torn,
Celebrating and partying; there was no need to mourn
They shared out their rations and partied in the street,
Beggars, children, rich men and thieves all came out to greet
Each other, no matter faith, nationality or race.
Humans, one after another, came together in a commonplace.

Celebrations were happening on that day alone,
For life went on, new seeds were sown.
Then, life was back to normal, days passed one after another.
For 364 days, the soldier became a husband, father and brother.

But that one special victory day,
That all of us remember in early May,
The heroes of the war that played their part,
Big, small or medium; they risked limb and heart.

Without them, we could be speaking German,
They were strong, resilient and definitely determined.
So honour them as this is their day,
In their medal-coated uniform celebrating away.

Prakrith Rao (13)

The World

On the streets of a city,
Down an endless row of flats,
You'll see never-ending traffic
And helpless stray cats.

Deep into the jungle,
There are wonderful sights you wish to seek,
Like monkeys swinging through trees
Or a beautiful toucan showing off its beak.

Through the deep, dark woods,
You might just discover,
A vulnerable flightless bird
Chirping for its mother.

Living on the savannah,
On the huge African plains,
Host fierce but proud male lions
Dwelling across the lands with their prominent manes.

In the very depths of the ocean,
There's a good chance you'll find,
Different species of undiscovered
Sea creatures, you can't even picture in your mind.

Even higher than the mountaintops,
Scattered amongst the great blue sky,
An admirable migrating flock of
Majestic eagles have just set out to fly.

Even in Antarctica,
A place where one will experience the coldest weather,
There are vast groups of penguins
Keeping warm by huddling together.

Beneath the earthly surface,
Digging tunnels underground,
Lives a very poorly sighted mole
Having to rely on touch and sound.

We may never come to have explored the whole planet,
We still haven't discovered a lot,
The best thing to do now is to
Sit back, relax and enjoy what we've got.

Robert Junior Arthur (15)

Sweet Bonds Of Life

Dreams with wings enfolded by the moonlight
Hope with wishes fill the sky

Beautiful memories fall like snow
Icicles melting with my feelings
See the bonds of hearts

The bonds that hold the emotions
Bonds that won't break
Different bonds of hope with different colours
They are strong enough to be what they are

Flowers bloom in the daylight
Day turns into night
Stars glisten in the nightlight
Earth comes to life

Dreams of tonight
Wishes of tomorrow
The beautiful rain covers the earth
Its voice calm and peaceful
My heart is tranquil

Birds sing in the midst of summer
Wind gushes through the mountains
The river glides with the waves of the ocean

The light and darkness of the sky
Fills the beauty of roses
In the vast time,
Roses bond with the wind of the earth

My heart that beats
With every crimson leaf that falls
Fills the sky with mesmerising emotions
Emotions that are felt once in a lifetime

The silence of time
Felt within the bonds of nature
Carve its path to freedom
Freedom of peace

Memories sealed amongst the night
Voices filled with emotions
Cascading into the light

Melodious whispers of the seasons
Wishes of tomorrow
Collide with the sweet bonds of life.

Kashaf-Ul-Noor (18)

The Best Thing That Happened To Me...

Small like a bee,
Heart as big as a great oak tree,
He's my little brother, the best thing that happened to me.

He rises in the morning,
After a long night of snoring,
Down the stairs he comes running,
Straight into my outstretched arms he comes hopping,
He's my little brother, the best thing that happened to me.

On a chair he lays wiggling,
Legs up in the air squiggling,
Arms above his head giggling,
My fingers tickling!
He's my little brother, the best thing that happened to me.

Outside my door, he's lurking,
After hours and hours of roaring and roaring,
A second of silence is all I'm asking!
Right into my room he comes cascading,

For warm hugs just like a little monkey smiling,
He's my little brother, the best thing that happened to me.

I love you oh so much,
The little things such and such,
Like how you eat your lunch,
Like a hamster you munch, munch, munch,
He's my little brother, the best thing that happened to me.

Thank you for being the best brother,
Even though I can sometimes be a bother,
You are like no other,
The best little bear-hugger,
Yes, you're my little brother, the best thing that happened to me.

Marian Herath (17)

Shadows And Streetlights

A swarm of cars buzz past speaking words of tranquillity
The hissing heard as I feel myself shift in bed between thoughts
Just on the outskirts, maybe a centimetre away from reality
A feeling that's found but rarely sought

The honey streetlights oozing through the ajar blinds
And the smell that comes from feeling like the only one awake
The light flickering next to me, almost by design
Just glad to feel what I feel, albeit an ache

Something so deep down, it could be in the skies
There's a quality to thinking in riddles that keeps me at ease
A maze of smiles and tears hidden behind these eyes
This moment so familiar, daytime might as well be overseas

Relishing the taste of my own pondering
Unknown to how long before I'm met with the fuzz of sleep

The shadows and curves of my room, light and meandering
Stitching tonight into forever, or maybe just a memory to keep

The all-too-welcome unfamiliarity of 'maybe'
A time to let myself find things hidden by the curtains of daylight
But I feel my eyelids flicker as I let sleep claim me
There's just something so captivating about the ever-ephemeral midnight.

Yaana Mishra (14)

The Ocean And Me

The best time of my life,
You'd think it would be with someone else,
Sharing the same moment,
And smiling about it in years to come.

The best time of my life,
You'd think it would be something extravagant,
Skydiving into the everlasting sky,
Creating an epic story to tell to friends.

The best time of my life,
You'd think it would be captured in a photo,
Bringing back all the feelings once again,
Making the memory last forever.

But to me,
The best time of my life,
Was the moment I came alive again.

I was alone in the ocean,
Discovering the world around me,
As if I was the first person on Planet Earth.

I threw my arms up in the air,
Splashing the water as I went,

Where it danced above me,
And then fell back through my hair.

I ran against the waves,
Whilst a spark ran through my body,
Creating a thousand tiny fireworks.

I fell back into the sea,
And laughed.
I stood back up again,
And looked around.

All of a sudden,
I was in a brand-new world.

In my eyes,
It was never about having a grand story to tell,
It was about a feeling.

A sensation that made me feel,
Whole.

Kiera Thorpe (15)

O' Wanderer

Take a breath, o' wanderer and listen to the lively chatter of the birds,
And the trickling streams, pushing water into the tiny ponds of fish,
Listen, o' wanderer and understand that no trouble must be stirred,
Know that you must answer nature's call, its only pleading wish.

The chittering of the birds, the gurgle of the streams, the tiny, golden fish,
These must all be protected, o' wanderer, from all these careless people,
From machines that cough thick oil and clog the rivers' calming swish,
Do not trust these factories, for they are nothing but dangerous trouble.

By all means, o' wanderer, light your fire but be it sparse of matches?
By all means, o' wanderer, put up your tent but be it sparse of plastic?
By all means, o' wanderer, lay your sleeping bag but be it sparse of catches?
By all means, o' wanderer, put on your fancy clothing but be it free of elastic?

This beautiful world, o' wanderer, belongs to both everybody and nobody,
We must all take care of it and we must put the forests of the world at ease.

Safiya Khalid (12)

My Heart Leaped For Joy

My heart leapt for joy as I saw a rainbow in the sky,
And as I ran to the park I watched her colours fly by,
She followed the sun, she looked down at the pretty flowers,
And everyone knew she had all the power,
I loved watching her glide on her clouds,
And she would show off her colours being proud.

My heart leapt for joy when I saw my garden for the first time,
It had all sorts of plants, trees, flowers and lime
But the plant I liked most of all,
Was my beautiful cherry blossom tree which was quite tall
It was majestic, it was grand
It was the best of them all, the best in the land.

My heart leapt for joy as I saw the autumn forest,
It had so many flowers even more than you would find in a florist,
There was a shimmering stream that gurgled over rocks,
And the wind's whisper it would mock,
The beautiful fall leaves, colourful and crisp,
And when they skated down from the trees they would talk with a lisp.

My heart leapt for joy when I saw nature,
I felt the air of the warm breeze,
And I could see beauty everywhere in the lakes in the trees.

Gayatri Gadepalli (10)

An A-Z Of Parties!

A ge is changing every year,
B alloons will make the children cheer!
C andy can be good to eat,
D iscos are a special treat!
E ntertainment has begun,
F riends can join in with the fun!
G ames are played just for a while,
H appy faces laugh and smile!
I ce cream can be great to share,
J oy is shining everywhere!
'K ings' and 'queens' are running around, their
L ollipops fall on the ground!
M enus can be good to make,
N o one wants to forget the cake!
O range juice is on the list,
P resents just cannot be missed!
Q ueues of children can't wait to
R eceive a party bag or two!
S weets are great for any event,
T hank you cards, they must be sent!
U ncles and aunts can sing and dance,
V enues must be booked in advance!
W rapping paper goes in the bin,

X marks the spot of treasure to win!
Y ears will pass and we'll do it again, but
Z zzzs will be needed to recover by then!

Isabelle Borg

I Thought I Would Let You Know

Your mind is playing tricks on you, my dear
You're troubled by your voice
Gasping for air from your thoughts
Like you have much choice.

You're collapsed, my dear,
You've been dragged by your hair
While you think they mutter quietly
While you think they stare.

My dear, you are puzzling,
You are lost beyond the clouds,
Your mind is commencing war on you,
You are withering in the crowds.

I know it all hurts my dear,
You stand to be knocked out in one blow
But it will get better, I'm sure
My dear if I did it, you can too
I know.

You are still here my dear
You are thriving
You are new

You can heal and grow
And do everything you want to do.

So rise, my dear
Leave the ashes and the grey
Leave what they said behind
They are not welcome
They are forgotten
They are not for today.

Jemma Crane

The Miserable Life Of The Two Brothers

Time was buzzing as fast as a buzzing bee
In the gloomy afternoon all I could see
The clouds were frustrated and livid at me
Only if I could listen to what they were saying at me
As soon as I stepped in the orphanage centre
My legs shattered into pieces as my brother ran away
Walter Tull, Walter Tull
Why are you thinking of running away?

Tearful tears, tearing us apart

Only Claire knows how to put us back to one part
Me being fuming, frustrated, fearful
And made Walter shiver in tears

Out of nowhere, Walter pushed me to Dr Steveson's office

In my point of view
I see
Walter
Grabbing the maid's arm
And asking questions

Now I know, now I know
The truth is exposed
I'm getting adopted but what about
The poor Walter
Tull

Will he live without me?
I don't know
I don't know...

Ashmeet Kaur (10)

What Life Means

Life is like going on a walk
and getting lost on the way
It's like running through a field of flowers,
feeling the wind flow through your hair
And wondering how anything so simple can make you feel so great

Life has its rainy days
Sometimes they last too long,
sometimes not long enough.
But with rain or no rain, we must remember to smile
We must remember to laugh and to cry
and maybe talk for a while.

In the rain we dance
And in life we make mistakes
Though every second we can hate
we could also learn to change.
We could stop.

Hear the music,
understand the meaning
Fulfil your dreams, without ever dreaming
Fill your pages

full of wonders forbidden,
With all the melody of a song unwritten.

Life is cruel and kind without meaning
And we fight with arms just to shoot
aimlessly, with no aim or hope yet we hope for the best.
For with precious beginnings comes a worthy ending.

Beatriz Suarez (15)

Lockdowns Suck

We started okay, it was a bit of a bummer let's say,
Locked in our houses all day,
But we had some fun,
Lots of walks with Mum,
Green spaces were our sun...

Summer came and we were let out again.
School was over but friends kept us sane.
We didn't manage to holiday in Spain,
Camping in Dorset and fun in the Lakes was our only aim.

We went back to school thinking it was okay,
Then lockdown came again and we weren't allowed to play.
It was cold by then and very mundane,
Locked in our houses day after day

Christmas came and went and that was fun.
Fireworks at night and a new year had begun.
Then months of home learning and finally a return
Our last year of primary and back to learn.

Slowly things became more fun
Everything sort of back to normal and no more walks with Mum.
Now I'm ready to start high school and I hope it's fun!

Jessica Carroll (11)

Stones Of Flesh

To climb a mountain
I dig my foot into ground
Stones move aside
Those who don't lay drowned

To ascend to the top
I lay a path of prints
To know where I was
So I can count my sins

But don't misunderstand
No weight lays on my back
For this is the way of the world
It's a cynical tone of black

Before you cast judgement
I pose you this
Do you care for the stones
That you prod and squish?

Do your actions match your ideals?
If not then you too are to blame
No matter what you say
You stepped on stones with no name

These stones are of flesh
May you watch them bleed
Squealing beneath your feet
While you speak on my greed

You and I are the same
We stomp on others to ascend
In a broken world
Unfixable, no way to mend

So to climb a mountain
How does one ascend
Without hurting a single stone?
Your journey's start is its end.

Isula Seneviratne (17)

Ten Penguins

Ten little penguins feeling fine, one fell over and then there was nine.
Nine little penguins all late, one got expelled and then there were eight.
Eight little penguins one called Evan, one slipped on ice and then there were seven.
Seven little penguins learning tricks, one made an explosion and then there were six.
Six little penguins taking a dive, one went under and then there were five.
Five little penguins heard a roar, one got scared and then there were four.
Four little penguins as clean as can be, one got dirty and then there were three.
Three little penguins one stepped in glue, one got stuck and then there were two.
Two little penguins had lots of fun, one fell asleep and then there was one.
One little penguin this is how it ends, goes back to the start and finds all his friends.

Rebecca Sade Bashorun (7)

Where Are Thou At 30?

Empowering the youth with words
Inspiring them to write
Publishing their work at no cost
Hosting amazing competitions
Rewarding writing talents
Making writing stars emerge
Wow! Young Writers:
You have motivated young people
You have encouraged them
You have made their voices to be heard, without separating the haves and the have-nots
You have created a platform for young people to share their work and experiences
Planted the love for writing within the young
So great are you like the proverbial Iroko Tree with many branches
Reaching out and supporting young people to attain their dreams
Finally, at '30' you have helped to achieve the sustainable development goals (SDG 4 - quality education) of the UN agenda 2030 target
Young Writers, you have really done well and need to be celebrated at 30 - Thumbs up!

Brinna Okechukwu (13)

The Four Seasons

The sun pelts the earth with a ray of light which
The children leave school to play in during summer.
The flowers are beautiful
Time begins speeding faster and faster.

The animals wander out in the world.
The last month of summer signals the return to an old friend
The last plant bears fruit.
Time begins to slowly calm down and fall in pace.

The final three-month rotation has begun.
The burning sun cools away into a soft caressing star.
The end of twelve months has come in autumn.
Time has completed one full year.

The snow falls from the sky
The ground becomes smothered in white
The water turns into ice
The tree branches become icicles
Spring is here in the air
You can smell it coming
On the trees,
Leaves are green
Busy bees are humming

These are the four seasons of the year
All are special, enjoyable and seasonal.

Daniel Ogundipe (12)

I Love The Seasons

I love the seasons
I love the seasons.

I love spring with its cute little bunnies,
I love autumn with its fiery glow,
I love summer with its fun beach days,
I love winter with its powdery snow.

I love making daisy chains with all my friends
and watching plants flower into bloom.
I love all the animals coming out to play
and birds harmonising at dawn.

I love leaves crunching under my feet as I walk,
and itching for Halloween.
I love dressing up in crazy costumes,
and collecting sweets as a team.

I love lying on the beach, playing with sand,
and going for a dip in the sea.
I love having crazy water fights with my friends,
and enjoying our summer holidays.

I love making snowmen out on the lawn,
and drinking hot chocolate inside.

I love wearing a big furry coat to stay warm, and opening presents by the fire.

Kheevi Harcourt (13)

The Zoo

Stomp, stomp, stomp go the charging feet
Rustle, rustle, rustle as they eat the crunchy leaves
Dig, dig, dig goes the rhinos' horns

Reach, reach, reach as they grab the hanging vines
Munch, munch, munch as they enjoy some tasty bananas
Chase, chase, chase as the monkey likes to play

Snore, snore, snore as they love to sleep
Pounce, pounce, pounce as they jump to their feet
Roar, roar, roar as the lion is the king

Waddle, waddle, waddle as they walk along the ice
Splash, splash, splash as their flippers swim around
Gulp, gulp, gulp as the penguin swallows the fish.

Long, long, long is the neck of this elegant animal
Black, black, black is the colour of their tongue
Dangle, dangle, dangle goes the giraffe legs.

Stephanie Green (7)

The Song Of The Seasons

There are four seasons in a year which each carry a song and hope.

There's the spring with a beautiful air that lurks about its ways
And the soft, sandy summers which rolls into the bay
The leafy autumn with a gentle sad breeze
And the dreary and drab winters, swinging on a temperamental trapeze.

There's the spring with the beautiful air
And the soft, sandy summers which are lovely when it isn't bare
The leafy autumn with the melancholic breeze
And the dreary and drab winters swinging on the trapeze

But people are mistaken.
There aren't only four seasons.
There are two more that are within reason.

There is also the stunning monsoon, with the rain as warm and relaxing as a hot, steaming shower
And the luscious prevernal that carries the hushed awakening of the animals and flowers.

Pranshi Gupta (12)

Party Popping Time!

The sun is shining,
The day is bright,
The birds are singing,
It all feels right

Yet no time to stop
Or take a lungful of air
The preparations are not done,
But party time is almost there!

Hurry, hurry, hurry!
Quick, quick, quick!
Rush around, don't lie about,
All the boxes on the list
Do need a tick!

Now, where were we...?
Oh yes!

Balloon-blowing
Bunting-hanging
Napkin-folding
Glowstick-snapping
Drum-banging
Card-making

Present-wrapping
All these things are overlapping

Getting all her favourite things,
Celebrating all she brings,
To this world,
Streamers unfurled.

Get the picnic rug out,
Stop lazing about!
She's almost here!
Lights out!

Pause...

Surprise, party!
Happy birthday!

Look at the smile on her face,
As she rushes to embrace!
The best day ever,
Will last forever!

Jessica Vali-Tsang (13)

The Soul Of The Dragonfly

I'll fly up there today,
Where the birds will sing away.
I'll watch, my eyes peeled
At the people that persevered.

Sitting on that dry-like land,
Eating all that it revealed,
And the birds would fly astray,
Taking insects on the way.

I will fly behind them all,
Waiting for the day to go.
But today is the day,
When I want to stay and play.

Flying into a house,
No mouse did dare squeak,
No insect did dare cry out.
It was all deathly silent for a house.

Then again the trap was sprung,
The spider weaved its net of fame.
And people came rushing in,
Taking me to the garden.
And I flew into the sky,

My wings a-beat,
My heart a-fly.

I waited until they were gone,
Then sat down and took a sigh.
Flapping my wings until they tired.
Going up and up, higher and higher,
Until dawn made me smile.

Vitaly Rassomakin (10)

Friends

Many people will walk in and out of our life
But only true friends will leave footprints in our life
To handle ourself we use our head
To handle others we use our heart
Anger is one letter short of danger
Great minds discuss ideas
He who loses money loses much
But he who loses friends loses much more
Us beautiful young children are the next generation of nature
But beautiful old people are works of nature
We learn from the mistakes of others
Friends Delicia, Izaac, George, Aleah - you and me
You brought another friend
And then there were more
We started our group
Our circle of friends
And like the circle
There is no beginning or end
Yesterday is history
Tomorrow is a mystery
But today is a gift.

Nabil Suleman (7)

The Words In His Hands

The boy who writes poetry...

You think you know the type,
Rich father, sophisticated mother,
An all-round nice life,
You know the type.

The one at the back of the class,
Secret brown notebook in hand
He writes everything he sees, hears and smells
On this land

Now that's not the type of boy who really understands
The power and expression behind the words in his hands
His words come from a thesaurus but not from his heart.
He treats poetry as a finely taught art

Do you still think you know the boy who writes poetry?

For, he doesn't sit in smoky French cafés
Because the whirr of the machine helps him think,
He sits alone in his bed, covering his eyes, on the brink...

Rachel Wilkinson (15)

Oblivion

Deep in the amusements of Alton Towers
Lies a ride that sends chills and thrills down your gutters

  O utermost ride
  B riskly going down
  L anky and leggy
  I ntimidating and hair-raising
  V erticle and vast
  I deal for thrill-seekers
  O utrageously accelerating
  N ifty and nimble

Up, up, up on a 65ft chain
Going slow towards the 88-degree drop
The ride has stopped
Is it broken?
No...
Argh!
Down the cart goes, with many screaming beings
Into a big, black hole
Later, exiting the pitch-black ditch and going at prolonged speeds

A few moments after that, the wonderful ride had sadly ended
What a journey that was, scary but splendid.

Sally Shammaa (10)

Celebrate Christmas

C hristmas is my favourite time, eating chocolate and cakes with family of mine.
E ach of my friends receives a card. Which is written straight from my heart.
L ove is all around in every city and every town; through all cultures, all creeds and each of the faces that we see.
E verlasting love touching us, like snowflakes falling from above.
B ells are ringing, church choirs singing. Presents arrayed to celebrate this day.
R udolph's hoofs springing and sprinting, through the night we share; that Christ's birth brings to rejoicers everywhere.
A ngels guided us to the sight, where Jesus lay below the nights light.
T ogether sat at a table on this special day.
E ast, west, south and north, everybody's love is shared to all.

Lily-Eden Bayliff (7)

Patterned Seasons

Sunny and rainy, it is spring
Birds are flying and singing
Gorgeous spring
Animals come out of hibernation and look for food
Plants grow like shooting stars
Farmers grow beautiful crops

Hot summer
Pollen from our gardens are stolen by bees
To see precious plants we go to the garden
Ducks swim around and around like a clock

When autumn rises, all the leaves fall down and down
All the plants wither step by step
The days get shorter and darker
The weather is wet and cold

Snow falls, ice slips, winter has come
Animals sleep and sleep
Snowballs and snowmen are everywhere
Everybody is excited for Christmas
Jingle bells, jingle bells, jingle all the way
Ho, ho, ho!

Shiyam Thulasiraj (8)

Corona

Oh corona, sweet corona,
how dare you ruin us all,
for many have died, some locked and survived,
but it truly is our fall.

For many of us, jobs have been lost,
which has put the country at great loss.
But we thank and salute those who continued to work hard,
like the NHS who stood strong like bodyguards.

Many think a vaccine will come soon,
but let me tell you this isn't a cartoon.
We will have to see in the years to come,
the thought of this makes me quite numb.

Tomorrow school will finally start,
but I don't think that's very smart.
Everyone's going to get very ill,
and no one's going to have a pill.

I wonder what our future will be,
I guess we'll have to just wait and see.
Will corona leave us alone?
The answer to this is purely unknown.

Khalil Daud (13)

Fireworks Are Cool

F ireworks, fireworks, such a beautiful sight to see!
I lluminating the night sky, they fill me with glee
R ed, yellow, green and blue
E xploding, blazing - wow what a view!
W hy can't this night just go on forever?
O h fireworks, fireworks - never stop, never!
R apidly soaring into the sky. They
K eep on going so fast!
S low down! Don't forget to say 'bye'!

A wesome indeed! Just look at them go
R ed, orange, green and yellow
E ven the aliens love watching the show!

C rowds of people, yelling and cheering
"O oh!" "Wow!" "Woah!" That seems to be the
O nly thing we're all hearing! Oops!
L ots more to see! Sorry, got to go!

Shamaila Khan (13)

Positivity

One candle can brighten the world,
with a nice smile that lifts up your soul.
Mix and grab your negative thoughts.
Shred them to pieces and leave a collection of positive thoughts that can be given to all.
Remember happiness is infectious, so bless everyone by smiling.
Your bright thoughts are powerful enough to drown your dark thoughts.
Never underestimate who you are and display positive vibes, like the rays of the sun.
The power of your positive rays will burn out your negative thoughts and feelings
Misery and sorrow dies and goes in the past when you only look at positive smiles.
You will always succeed if you be yourself and never give up
If you remember what I said you will achieve extraordinary things and always remember, kindness is free.

Maryiam Tajdin (12)

Today

As the nights go younger
and my days longer,
the day of torment is right around the corner.
Again, I have to go through this brutal torture

Didn't know the days of freedom would go that quick
now all I can hear is the clock going tick,
the day of torment is right around the corner.
Again, I have to go through this brutal torture.

The fear of the same routine and stress just
made everything in my head a mess,
the day of torment is right around the corner.
Again, I have to go through this brutal torture.

The day came closer and closer
as for my days, they became slower and slower,
the day of torment is right around the corner.
Again, I have to go through this brutal torture.

I went to bed - it was my last day.
Woken up as there I lay.
It was today.

Izza Khan

Nature

Nature is a beautiful wild atmosphere,
Where the flowers thrive freely as well as the deer,
The trees tower over you and the grass is lush green,
The dew sparkles gently and is as bright as Showsheen,
Birds call to each other from the treetops and hedges
And you wonder if they're making any promises or pledges,
Hedgehogs and rodents roam the moss-coloured floor
And are scared by all predators and many more,
Daisies and clover bloom in various places
And wild horses move around in their fast, flashy paces,
Caterpillars turn into butterflies as nature evolves,
While any worry or problem slowly resolves,
Nature is verdant, loving and kind
And this relaxing environment is very rare to find.

Alice Watson (10)

Stationery Upgrade

I once had a pencil that could write and draw
all by itself, although, really was a bore.
it drew the Mona Lisa and the Last Supper too,
but one day for no reason at all
out of my window, it flew.

But then I found an eraser and all my mistakes had gone!
This might run away too! I have to hold on!
I stayed a whole week with my magical eraser
but then it ran away!
off with the pencil might I dare say

I got fed up with stationery both magical and normal
so in school, my writing wasn't very formal
I'd thrown away my pencils, erasers, and all
I only wrote with a pen that on its end had a tiny ball.

So the moral of this story
the meaning at the end
don't trust stationery in all of their glory
rely on your pen, now that's a good friend.

Favour Adeyonu (11)

A Day At The Beach

Waves crashing along the shore,
This is a sound I will always adore,
Making me happy and calming me down,
However, also hoping that I don't drown.

Watching seagulls fly high in the sky,
Didn't think I would find them in Dubai,
Turning to the left and seeing the tallest building,
It's very, very true - I'm not kidding.

Two girls run across the bach,
Running at me I sense a smell of a peach,
I turn around and see a fish,
Suddenly, I really want it as my dish.

Then I see the time and now I have to leave
I have to leave the beach and go have dinner with my uncle Steve
Because of this I am kind of upset
But at least I got to see the sunset!

Alicia Cimpoeru (13)

Celebrate, Celebrate!

C elebrate, celebrate, celebrate - we all celebrate special occasions
E very year we celebrate Islamic New Year, Eid Ul-Adha, Eid Ul-Fitr and Ramadan
L et's celebrate all occasions by wearing new clothes and eating delicious, yummy food
E very day we pray five times a day
B e nice and kind to everyone you meet as they will remember you for a lifetime
R eady for all special occasions and welcoming your guests
A t all times in your life be nice and kind to everyone you meet as they will remember you
T o celebrate each occasion with my family is special
E at yummy, delicious food and carry on celebrating all the special occasions all the time.

Muhammad Umar Abbas (8)

Long Ride

An isolated row of seats,
Severely scuffed and bruised.
Caked in layers of dust and grime,
Longing to be used.

Scarlet paint on dented metal,
Slowly flaking and peeling away.
From the outside barren landscape,
Torn newspapers, fluttering astray.

Musty smells of gas and petrol,
Lingering in the air.
Rush of passengers and children,
Extremely, very rare.

Apart from a peculiar lone figure,
Reading, eyes darting across the page.
Gripping onto the vehicles pole,
Grubby and rusted with age.

Her lips curled into a smile,
As she gave me an unfathomable look.
And adjusted her small, round hat,
Turning the page of her battered book.

Moving clouds in the sky,
Slowly obscured the sun.
The creaky bus lurched forward,
And the long ride had begun.

Sophia Popova (13)

Flying Shuttlecocks!

I walk into the court feeling proud,
I hear the crowd cheering out loud.

I win the toss, I choose my side,
I stare across the other side.

The whistle blows,
The game starts.

My opponent hits and I give back,
And on it goes whack after whack.

I win the game but
There are three to play.

Sweat is dripping down my face
And my feet are on fire.

I want to win not lose,
The thought of loss is dire.

The next game begins,
I run and run until one would collapse.

It is worth it, I step on the stage,
With a gold medal around my neck.

I look at the crowd to see,
Smiling faces looking up at me.

Aaliyah Ali

The Awakening

The ice in the cave
Frozen with despair
Awaiting
Cries crowding in on each other
Dark and light meet

Connection
Bound by the very essence of life
Piercing of the seven
Starlight, that is
Pure and solid
The mist of fury and love mix

Combination so bright it hurts
Pain that strikes through the veins
Pumping into the very stream
It compels you to insanity

Betrayal to a kingdom
Discovery of the heart
How can this soul go on?
To betray or not to betray

Difficulty is what strives the heart
Stars twinkling in the sky light

Moonlight dancing above
Universe answering the untold

Spirits colliding
A newly discovered gem
Gleaming in the night sky
The prince of darkness has awakened again

Thorn in hand
What shall it do to life?

Alara Kunacav

My Enchanted Embrace

The crisp ocean comforts my toes,
The wet sand burying my feet,
I feel as if I am in motion,
But I investigate and find that I am still.

The chucking and washing hugs my ears,
The wind glides over my cheeks,
The novelty of being here again never subsides,
And the salty freshness aroma raises my heart.

The golden blanket in which I seek comfort,
Is always warm and locks me in,
The castles, the holes and the mountains,
All participate in the recurring nostalgia.

I gaze at the scenery lying before me,
The blended watercolours in the sky,
The gold and cobalt-blue base,
And for another year, I leave this enchanted embrace.

Sidra Malik (15)

Mount Everest

The tallest mountain in the world
The tallest mountain in the world...
What could it be?
Where the winds hurl and twirl
And where it's -42 degrees

It's a massive 8,848 meters tall
It's over 60 million years old
Be careful not to fall
Or you'll die from the cold

The winds go a whopping 175 miles per hour
Faster than the mighty cheetah
Look at that immense power
Brrrrrr! It is cold here, any spare heater?

Sir Edmund Hillary was first to climb the mountain on May 29, 1953
What an achievement that occurred
Finally he was done and free
He was so joyful and assured

The tallest mountain in the world
What could it be?
Where the winds hurl and twirl
It's Mount Everest, you can't disagree.

Mohammed-Ayaan Iftikhar (10)

Chickens

In their coop, my chickens love to roam.
It makes me happy to see them at home.

I love the way they peck and cluck
And lay some eggs if I'm in luck

For a tasty egg is my favourite treat,
Into the mixing bowl, give it a beat!

There are many ways it can be used.
They really do make me amused!

Fried, scrambled or boiled,
I truly am spoilt!

An ingredient for a delicious cake!
Or other things I like to bake!

On a spoon, in a race,
Just be careful! Slow your pace!

In a nursery rhyme, sat on a wall,
Humpty Dumpty, please don't fall!

As an Easter gift, who would have thought?
That eggs would be that kind of sort!

I dream of the wonders my chickens lay,
And then, *splat!* Oh No, not today!

Martha Pearson (11)

The Forest

Little flower buds
Even if no one can see
Open anyway

The ambitious crow
We see a twig in her beak
But she sees a home

From a great distance
Branches pierce the sapphire sky
Like dark lighting bolts
But branches up close
Will tell another story
One of potential

If you look closely
You can find marvellous things
That yearn to be seen

If you look closer
You might find something hidden
Deep in the shadows

Which one of these are we?
Shall we hide or shine bright?
We cannot do both

We are very small
But the things inside our hearts
Could fill up the sky.

Cacper Dzieminski (11)

Cookies And Cupcakes

Cookies and cupcakes are like my two best friends
one has my favourite sprinkles
and one has my favourite icing
I don't know what I would do without them.

I love cookies and I love cupcakes
who knows what they would taste like together
they may have something in common.
Cookies taste like a delight mixed with your favourite candy
and cupcakes are like a rainbow mixed with a candyfloss cloud
but you should never have too much
because in your head, it will be loud!

I have not got a clue
about what I would do
without my two
BFFs!

Cookies are the best
and cupcakes are the best
but now I need a rest!

Ameerah Adil Salim (11)

My Poem About Christmas

Christmas is more than just a day in December
It's one of those special days we love to remember
Snow falls from the sky
As Santa and his reindeer go by
The smell of Christmas fun was up in the air
And nothing seemed bare
Everyone was happy, everyone was jolly
Bannisters were decked with boughs of holly
And the Christmas songs play
People's sadness quickly faded away
Cookies were baked
Cakes were caked
Wrapping paper was scattered all over the carpet
People got comfortable in their blanket
Christmas time was finally here
Laughter, singing and rejoicing was heard in every neighbourhood
I love this time of year!

Annicha Djiele (12)

Lightning Dog

My name is Rooney
My mate's name's Moony
Let me tell you my story
With some of my friends

It was thunder and lightning
I was playing
I went toilet outside
My mate looked at the tide

Lightning struck
I tried to duck
I got rushed to the hospital
Outside the mall

Next day we went to Tori's lab
She told me to blab
She got me suited and booted
I scooted

I am lightning dog
I went through the fog

"I've been robbed!" yelled a dog
I ran from the bog
Kicked the bad guy's butt

Sent him to a hut
Got rewarded
I got recorded.

Sukhveer Bhangu (11)

The Perfect Cup Of Hot Chocolate

The perfect cup of hot chocolate
Is like an old best friend,
It's sweet, so elite and such a treat!
Fulfilling till the end,
Can't wait until we meet again.

The cup of hot chocolate,
Rich and chocolatey it is,
Amazing memories never forgotten,
If there were twelve cups full
I could drink the lot.

The surface is covered in
A swirly hill of cream,
On top of a marshmallow mound,
Seemingly enjoying dancing around,
Eventually vanishes without a sound.

But there's a warning to it,
Like careless words in a friendship,
Or impudently rushing to judge,
Alas, you would feel the prick!

Karen Alexy (12)

Our Wondrous Nature

Nature! Nature! So lush and green
The wonders of wonders anyone has ever seen
So cool, calm and full of life
Makes us forget about all our strife
Think of a forest full of trees
Fluttering and dancing in the breeze
Trees we cut and construct towers
Lives are killed in mere hours
The birds that soar so high in the sky
We can't even imitate them however hard we try
We learn to be astounded and gaze at things
And see the happiness that it brings
Normally at trees, axes we swing
Instead let's do what we can to save a wing
So children in the future
Can see what we have nurtured.

Kuhu Rajadhyaksha (12)

Paddy Chonk

Fond eyes stare at me,
holding me tight from
across the room.
Without any words
So much can be said;
Each statement an amalgamation
of simply words I desire.
All so convincingly truthful.

Soft fur presses against me!
Insulating me from
any troubles.
While it may be impossible
to discern right from wrong
in any scenario;
It's so easy to trust one's judgment
when only one point of view
can be voiced.

Man's best friend is
Seemingly a friend to anyone
with a piece of cheese.
But I refuse to accept
that if everyone held a block

he would run to anyone
except me.

I never intend to find out
however,
Because Paddy tells me
I'm the only huwman he luwvs.

Oliver Hard (16)

That Place

There's a place
Not much like the rest,
There are no swimming pools
No theatres,
No golf course or
Aeroplane landing in the back.

Instead,
There are shouts from voices so familiar,
Shadows that merge as their owner's embrace,
Smells of comfort and acceptance.

Down the corridor,
A figure stands,
Reading the news,
Beer in hand.

Up the stairs,
Two figures fight
About what television programme to watch.
One wants cartoons,
The other frowns,
It seems they never agree on anything.

To the right,
A woman folds,

The foreign clothes,
Her child brought back,
Smiling as she realises how quick time has passed.

This is a place I'll never forget.

Annika Tang

It's All The Same

The days of summer are drifting away,
Autumn starts; the leaves red, orange but not grey,
Raking of the fallen; admiring of the tall
Admiring of the tall trees that look down from above,
Waiting for winter when people give nothing but a cold shoulder; a shrug
It goes from being at home at eight to having to be home at five,
You don't know what is out there, we are all trying to survive,
Trying to survive the shivers autumn or winter may bring,
Hearing the birds sing and listening to the whistling wind
As it sweeps up the fallen leaves from tall trees that people admire,
I believe as summer ends, autumn starts and winter awaits,
It's all the same.

Emmratu Blango

Old Friends

Rimmed wheels rattling on ageing steel tracks,
The numbing moan of an old engine labouring along,
The squealing hum of a pantograph on cables overhead,
Singing loudly as we pass underneath.

Bodies shake as we advance down the route,
With an increase of speed, the wind gushes around us,
Chilling our faces, fixing our smiles,
Bells ring to alert others of our presence as we trundle onwards down the track.

The clink clunk of the regulator controlling our descent,
Old brakes ease us to a stop at our destination,
Ready to board another service,
At the Tramway Museum at Crich.

Morgan Davidson (14)

Polar Bear

Sleek white fur, invisible against the pure frozen landscape
Soft padding of paws whisked away by the icy wind
An invisible predator stalks downwind
Concealing its scent, as it does itself

Pawprints to remain undiscovered
Snow washing over them like a gentle wave
Obscuring them from view

The concealed bear leaps from the snow
Teeth tearing the carcass of its unlucky victim
After eating its fill the deadly, powerful assassin slinks away
Melting into the icy plains

All that remains is the blood of its prey slowly soaking into the once pure snow
Without a trace the powerful, deadly, silent polar bear
Has vanished into the Arctic snow.

Dylan Watson (11)

The Calming Places We Go To

Walking, walking, walking
I walk when I need to relax
When I need to feel at peace with myself
I let my feet take me wherever they feel necessary
The music playing so loudly in my ears I can barely hear my surroundings
And when I walk, I always pass the park
the park
Where everyone goes to play, run, walk, or talk
I see these people smiling, talking or even just people sitting quietly and I feel at ease
Like all the stress and negative energy has drained from my tense body
Tranquillity taking over
And I know that this is my calming place.

Corlene Mazwi (15)

Witches' Brew

For a babbling beverage,
Mix yolks and jokes,
For a giggling charm,
Add cream and dreams,
For a tongue-twist potion,
Tip some tricks,

For a levitation spell,
Sip knowledge and college,
For a truth cup,
Mix lies and ties,
For a tickling curse,
Add nails and tails,

For a defying potion,
Add bark and lard,
For a sluggish spell,
Mix slugs and bugs,
For an invisible brew,
Tip some tips,

For a summoning charm,
Add bits and lids,
For a healing cup,
Mix plasters and laughter,

For a pumpkin jinx,
Add seeds and leads,

For a water-breathing potion,
Mix sea and weed,
For this poem to end,
Read till the end!

Rania Pannun (10)

The Jungle Beat

Swishing through the forest
What is that I hear?
Birds singing, bees humming, tigers prowling?
With a definite jungle beat.

Swishing through the forest
What is that I hear?
Gnarled roots crackling, big, bad badgers digging
Or maybe a man sneezing?

Swishing through the forest
What is that I hear?
Crocodiles snapping, rhinos bellyflopping?
But wait, what is that I see?

The sun shimmering on a beast,
A dancing dino and his friends
Out of the forest and back to the start
Shaking to the jungle beat.

Joshua Alexy (8)

Birthday Bash

It's a poetry party, come celebrate!
It's a poetry party, show no hate!
It's a poetry party, let's dance all day long!
It's a poetry party, let's sing a song!
There's ice cream, confetti, there's music too,
There's dancing, drinks, and a unicorn that flew!
There's cake, party hats, presents too,
It's a world of fun, you should come too!
It's Young Writer's 30th, what to get?
Maybe a book, they'll like it, I bet!
The party has ended, it was very fun,
I must go because the day is done!

Nona Nwajide (8)

The Word Party

C heeky words play tricks, hop around and giggle,
E lephant-sized words stomp about, as mice-shaped ones scamper underneath,
L ying in a heap, lazy words slouch about and scoff cake,
E veryone watches out for piping hot words: they are coloured burnt red!
B ut leafy words are not concerned as they sit on the rafters, rustling quietly, watching
R ude words bellow insults and smirk
A nd shy words will not dare to complain, they shrink into corners while
T he joyful, kind words give out sweets and roses.
E very word shall celebrate!

Esmee Raghavan (10)

Visit To The Restaurant

I smartly stepped over the threshold,
Onto the burnished wooden floor.
In the blink of an eye,
A waiter came to my aid and gave me a tour.
I sank into a chair wrought of a glistening white metal,
Laid splendorously in front of me were plates, glasses and sparkling cutlery beyond measure.
Suddenly, waiters glided over the smooth floor,
Bringing steaming platters,
Piled high with seafood, all scrumptious.
I consumed the various courses ravenously until I was full to the brim,
That was the best dinner I had had in many a year.

Hasan Suruliz (9)

It's Summertime!

Time's ticking
Summer is waiting
Let's just jump into the pool

Eating too much ice cream
Drinking too much lemonade
Spending too much time outside
Come on, it's summertime

Hearing all the warm waves
Feeling all the soft sand
Eating all the incredible ice cream

Smelling all the sticky sweat
Seeing all the crazy crabs
This is what summer plans

Enjoying our holidays
Relaxing almost every day
Everyone is now excited
Because now...
It's summertime!

Manreet Kaur (11)

When You See A Poppy Field

When you see a poppy field
Red petals tossed in dance
Green grass growing prim and neat
On which a deer might prance.

There was a time when poppy fields
Were filled with sludge and mud
The only sign of colour
Was the sight of trickling blood.

The hedge beaten down and worn
Barbed wire tangled up
The mangled sight of bodies
In prayer the hands are cupped.

So when you see a poppy field
Remember the terrified soldiers
Remember them and honour them
For they shall not grow older.

Daniel Leaver (13)

NHS The Brave

Bravely they charge into war
Bravely smiling and so much more
Bravely walking through that door
Bravely not knowing what is in store
Bravely succeeding one by one
Bravely may I add, succeeding with my broken collar bone
Bravely being kings and queens of the war
Bravely supporting us all one and all
Bravely tripping the virus until it no longer stands
Bravely we are cheering for you
Hip, hip hooray
Go NHS, we are cheering for you
Bravely you were here for us
Now we are here for you
NHS - go, go, go!

Jaskaran Bhachu (11)

Birthday

C rumbly but delicious
A nd sometimes fruity too
K een to just bite into it
E at it all up with you

P artying all day long
R un, dance and play
E veryone's having fun
S o come join us today
E arrings from a present
N erf guns and books too
T hank you for my gifts
S o very kind of you

F abulous outfits all around
U nicorn balloons
N ext year can't come soon enough - happy birthday to you!

Mia Martin (7)

My Favourite Festival (Onam)

A flower decoration with a range of colours,
Sits in the middle of the courtyard,
The shapes stand out with contrasting pigments,
Beautiful patterns capture my eyes,
Whilst the people I love are gathered together, talking and taking photos,
Tempting food sits on the floor, waiting to be eaten,
Palm leaves filled with a variety of curries,
Sweet and sour, hot and cold,
My skirt drags behind me,
As a string of jasmines are draped above my hair,
Everyone bonds over funny memories and delicious desserts,
The excitement fades away,
Everyone leaves hours past midnight.

Prayaga Salim (10)

My Deadly Revenge

The day has ended
But not my feelings
I remember what happened and what they recommended
I am not attending any more meetings!

Now I am back
Back on my feet
Reality would be exposed
Knowing their heart is black
My desire and destination now will be completed!

The time has come, time to defeat
Everyone will be watching on the street
I don't care what people will say
Now it's their time to pay

They will regret it by crying and screaming
As I take my deadly revenge.

Harman Doll (14)

My Mother's Perfume

The hills above are silent,
Where the flowers dance in tune,
The daffodils and lilies,
Smell like my mother's perfume.

It only took a second,
For them to be in my clutch,
And make her happy again,
Because I love her so much.

I made my potion,
And mixed it all together,
Full of my hopes and dreams,
For me to endeavour.

A spray bottle held,
The richness of the field,
It's purity and greatness,
I had concealed.

For only one step I had to take,
Was in the grand bedroom,
Where a lady would smile,
Because her daughter made her mother's perfume.

Megan Ceesay

Love

Love is so powerful
It's the feeling of joy
The feeling of a heartwarming hug from your most favourite person in the world
Love is so incredible
It's like having the most delicious meal
It's filling your stomach
It gives you the best feeling in the world
Love is so magical
It's like a feeling you can't imagine
It can appear from nowhere
Love is out of this world and is a spectacular power
It can make you happy on a sad day
It can lift you up when you're feeling down.

Leah Bashorun (10)

A Hero

You're not just my uncle.
You're not just a nurse.

You teach me to try my best,
Sometimes I do bad, sometimes I do good.
You show me everything is possible,
I say 'I can't', you say, 'you could'.

You fight to save life,
Sometimes you can't, sometimes they die.
You never doubt the decisions you make.
You comfort families when all they do is cry.

You're not just my uncle,
You're not just a nurse,
You're a hero in our universe.

Sophie Whitfield-Gray (12)

Happy

When I'm with my friends and family
Laughing and smiling cheerfully
Reminiscing old memories and past moments
These are the things that make me happy

Travelling, dancing
Playing, prancing
Being with people that love me dearly
These are the things that make me happy

Reading a book
Or writing in my notebook
Cooking up recipes
Or singing melodies
Always make me smile every time
These are the things that make me happy

Watching movies on the TV
Or listening to music on an mp3
It's always just the simple moments
That make me happy.

Daniella Analogbei (12)

Our Pandemic Heroes And Miracles

Vaccines are miracles
They make the future safe and bright,
Out of the dark COVID-19
We finally saw the light.
The scientists, doctors and nurses
Who really did care,
Made so many supplies
For the whole world to share.
The doctors and nurses worked so hard
For these two troublesome years,
They are the most courageous people
Who have no fears.
We must work together and pray
So that safe we may be,
The only way we can get out of this
Is if we think as We, not Me.

Subaha Falaq Chowdhury (11)

The Ferocious Weather

Sun, wind and beat of the sea,
Water stretching endlessly,
Smell the sea, feel the sky,
Let your soul and spirit fly,
no blue, no green,
no water, no life,
no sea, no land,

In a flash I heard a crash,
as the feracious sea explodes,
crashing and bashing against the rocks, little turtles in the sea,
trying to survive the feracious sea,

As the sun begins to rise,
The little turtle didn't realize,
The warmth was very touching,
As the sun was going down,
All the villages were filled with peace.

Gifty-Favour Thompson (8)

2054

My eyes are open,
My mouth is wide,
As I stare
Outside.

The roads are flooded,
No trees around,
The water is rising,
The trees were cut down.

Then I remember,
Silly me.
It's been like this
Since I was 33.

Scientists are trying
To help.
So people can live,
And animals as well.

But there's
No going back.

Only death,
Destruction,

Demise,
Demolition.

Only boiling,
Rising,
Tears,
Goodbyes.

Oxygen at 50%,
Carbon dioxide is high.

Death and destruction,
Demise, demolition.

No breath,
No happiness,
No...
Time.

Liela Richardson (12)

The Seasons

The seasons
Each one comes and each one falls

Spring, summer,
Autumn and winter,
These are the seasons,
Four in all.

Spring is the time for green and new life,
Where animals join the wildlife.
Summer days ahead and school days behind, this is the time to shine.
Autumn leaves fall and animals lay,
Sound asleep until New Year's Day.
Ice and snowfall, winter at last,
Soon to be a day in the past.

Spring, summer,
Autumn and winter,
These are the seasons,
Four in all,

Each one comes and each one falls.

Darcie Wright

It's Party Time

I am eight
T oday is great
S it with your mate

P erfect party, presents everywhere
A crobatic entertainment, seen it somewhere?
R ainbow-coloured balloons flying in the air
T wo teddy bears for the winner of musical chairs
Y ipee! Isn't it like a funfair?

T ime to have some fun
I ce cream for everyone
M agnificent costumes
E njoy yourself with the musical tunes.

Aiza Anwaar (8)

Change

Spring brings all the gold of nature's worth,
With its promise of new birth,
There are many rain showers,
And many long happy hours.

All the summer through,
The sun star shines on me and you,
Waves lap on the seashore,
On warm days walking is such a chore.

Autumn is revealed,
Beautiful leaves no longer concealed,
There are blackberries to pick,
But you better be quick.

Next comes winter with thunder and rain,
Only evergreen leaves remain,
It is cold and harsh outside,
So by the fire we must hide.

Caitlyn Irving (14)

Seasons

S pecial, each and every season unique and different.
E legant, the winter snow drifting down from the skies above.
A utumn, the season that embraces the colourful nature.
S ummer, that warm air shining through the white fluffy clouds.
O bedience, the dark clouds not disturbing our time with our family.
N ature, the key to our happiness, as well as the seasons
S pring, my favourite season of all as nature grows in a new form.

Shupany Sabesh (12)

My 15th Birthday Party!

My birthday party was amazing
Family and friends were embracing
People brought me gifts
People brought me presents
They were full of incredible surprises
Money, clothes etc

My birthday party was the best
But not better than the rest
Decorations more colourful than a rainbow
You could even say it was one of the best parties that I ever had!

Being 15 can be hard work sometimes
But if you trust yourself, nothing is hard!

Benjamin Doeteh (15)

Parties

Words can have so many meanings.
Those meanings too,
Have their own meanings,
Own memories,
Own experiences,
That change the meaning.

To someone a party
Is about wearing a backless dress,
Having the best time of their life,
No matter the address,
Whether they're with their brother or wife.

To someone else a party
Is just another thing that induces anxiety,
What to wear is impossible to decide,
For they're going to get judged by society
And embarrass themselves worldwide.

Vari Patel (14)

The Sea

Darting gracefully the seahorse left
his home on the colourful reef

It swam high above the shoal
of blue, yellow and red
spotted butterfly fish

In the coral, the territorial
angelfish kept watch
silently on the shark

Like a shark the sly angelfish
was stalking its prey
it waited patiently for the rival

The resident sea turtle
circled, swirled and swerved under
the huge blue whale.

Gilbert Phillips (8)

Dreams

I woke up from a wonderful dream
I was treated like a queen
I had everything I wanted
I had my wishes granted

I woke up from a nightmare
I was living the word scare
I saw someone in the distance
I looked a little closely and recognised her in an instance
Phew! I'm safe in my existence

"Wake up!" shouts my mum
The horror pops out of me like gum
I wish it was the dream where I was the queen.

Aiza Hussain (9)

Little Girl

I am only seven,
But I am the best,
Like at singing and dancing,
I will ace the test.

I love to do paintings,
Of flowers and fruit,
Every time I walk outside,
People say I am cute!

I am very strong,
Like my dad,
I try to be good,
So my parents don't get sad.

I wish I was a princess,
With a big castle and crown,
Maybe a knight in shining armour,
Or even a clown.

One day,
I will be the best in the world,
But for now,
I will be Mommy and Daddy's little girl!

Maiya Ceesay

Pigeon Fight

I saw two pigeons fighting in the park
Tufts of feathers were pecked from each bird.
The victor stood its ground, while the loser flew away and scowled from a tree.
I could hear an aggravated warbling emanating from the pair.
The exhaust from an old car spewed the stench of petrol everywhere.
I tasted the distinctive flavour of Irn-Bru.
My wet jacket clung to my shirt and would not let go.
I felt a strange sort of thrill as I'd never seen anything like it before.

Alasdair James Riddell (13)

It's A Special Day

It's a very special day,
Comes around every year
That day is now drawing near
We are learning how to write
And seeing the light
Oh how our creative minds are changing the world
We are showing our creative side
We are writing our work with pride
It shall soon be the birth of the day we begin to express ourselves
And the day people start picking up our books on the shelves
We start at a young age
We thrive and are engaged
Thanks for helping us reach for the stars.

Aretha Tsanga

Climbing The Mountain

Once I set off
On a journey aloft
Climbing high in the sky
1,085 metres
I climbed with three companions
My brother, my mammy and my grandad
When we finally got to the top...
Beautiful birds sung
A glider swayed as it zoomed through the air
Seagulls screeched
People laughed in joy as they got to the top
We had dinner up there
We put effort into every step
There stood Snowdon proud and tall
We climbed Snowdon
We climbed the tallest mountain in Wales
It was amazing!

Ryan Watson (9)

Dragons

Dragons are my favourite
Of all mythical creatures
Their colourful scales
Glow when the sun sets
When they are ready for flight
They spread their giant wings
Every dragon has their own magic
Some have fire, some have strength and some can shape-shift
Not all dragons have scales
Some are angel-like with feathery bodies and wings
Some are good
Some are bad
Whatever they do
They are still my favourite!

Jovita Kurilenko (12)

Love

A poem to be read backwards

Love is idyllic, intoxicating; immaculate.
There is no way that,
Love isn't the solution to all your problems.
Of course,
Love is sophisticated. Stylish. Snazzy.
I'd be lying if I said that,
Love isn't ubiquitous.
Like it says above,
Love is always there at all times.
It isn't true that,
Love is absurd, aggravating or asinine.
Undeniably,
Love is like a flower you've got to let grow.
It is false that,
Love is dumb or doomed, or even dead.

Chidimma Oguledo (14)

Alone

There is a time when we feel alone
We need our fathers but where did they go?

There is a time where we want to cry
We need our mothers but they are not there

There is a time when we feel angry
We need our brothers but they do not care

There is a time we just want to laugh
We need our sister but she's at her dad's

Alone, alone, where can they be?
Alone, alone, someone help me!

Rosie Roberts-Bridgewater (13)

The Seasons

There are four seasons in the year...

In spring flowers bloom
The weather is 10-18 degrees
Spring is March, April and May

Summer is the hottest season of the year
Weather is 19-30 degrees
Flowers grow
The school holidays start

Autumn is cold
Weather is 9-18 degrees
School resumes

Winter is cold
Weather is -1-10 degrees
Winter is December, January and February.

Abdullah Okelola (7)

The Taste Of A Party

Blanket of soft cream
The crackle of the candle
Glitch of colourful dots,

Punch of the OJ
The sizzling sour kick of it
Blueberries' bold blood,

Bounce of the gummy
Squishy pillow of sweeties
Drops of a rainbow,

The crunch of the crisps
A spicy smack - followed by
Then a sudden bliss,

And a wave of song - ripples across the room,
Light by light kickstarted by smiles,
The gentle tune gradually dissipates,
Hugging the voice's hearts.

Mia Gallacher (13)

A Season Called Summer

As I walk outside my house,
I smell the lovely air,
It smells so sweet like lavender.
Oh, I see a hare.

I skip up and down,
I look down the path.
Oh yes, summer is a beautiful place,
Where animals have a nice bath

Everything is emerald-green.
Yes, all those big, long trees.
And the beautiful flowers I see,
Are where the tiny little bumblebees be.

How I love it so much,
Hmm, such a bummer.
That it will always end,
This season called summer.

Simisola-Zion Ajibade (11)

I Am The Earth

I am the Earth,
I am your home,
I've been invaded, especially in Rome,
I am being polluted every day,
If this keeps up, I won't stay,
Animals are dying every day,
Global warming has to pay,
Otherwise humans won't stay,
Do me a favour, just this once,
And stop using fossil fuels from my crust,

I am the Earth,
I am your home,
I've been invaded, especially Rome.

Kavish Chavda (8)

Passion

My passion's what I owe
All my writings to,
'Cause passion is what makes me see
The world your eyes through.
My passion is my weapon,
That I cannot deny,
It's always been by my side
Through dark and any light.
It's made me confident
And helped me see
That something that you haven't tried
Its judge you cannot be.
To passion, my saviour
To passion, my friend
To passion who I know will be by my side,
Forever till the end.

Ermioni Tsantikou (11)

Happiness

Happiness is nice when
You have some fries.
Happiness is peace when
You are with your niece.
Happiness is kind when
You share something you find.
Happiness is sleeping when
You are dreaming.
Happiness is fun when
You are in the sun.
Happiness is writing when
You are not fighting.
Happiness is caring when
You are sharing.
Happiness is flying when
You are not lying.

Huda Ahmed (8)

The Art Of L'manburg

Once a land of laughter,
Once a land of love,
A man called Wilbur,
And his son and brothers he loved the most.

Many years later it was no more,
Now it's just a hole on the floor,

Many months later it began to bloom,
Of trees and bones and waterfalls began to fall,
The glass was removed and it shone in daylight and moonlight,
It was the art of a nation called L'manburg.

Millie Thornton (13)

The Lost Embrace Of My New Face

Hold me close and hold me tight
Don't be scared, it'll be alright
I am within you and you with me
Our memories will soon be free
Don't have fear to feel okay
And don't mind me as I disappear today
Oh I really wish I never did stay
My memories will soon fade away
As I stay back you can finally be released from this depression
I hope you'll feel free my new impersonation.

Zarah Khalifa (13)

Chocolate

Its rating takes debating
the taste is just great
after it finishes, you will always want more
it is something you will never hate

You can get it in all kinds of colours
but my favourite one is brown
you will always take it with a smile
and never with a frown

It really is so yummy
it is something I always eat
and that thing is none other than
delicious chocolate!

Maheen Fahad (11)

On The Farm

On the farm
The sky so blue
I hear the cows moo
On the farm
Never alarmed

Herding the sheep
I watch them as they leap
Shredding their wool
Their stomachs are always full

Feeding the chickens
How their wings thicken
They lay their eggs
Oh the chicklet's tiny legs

How the horses neigh
They love the month of May
They gallop on their feet
They look pretty neat

The sky so blue
I hear the cows moo
On the farm
Never alarmed.

Zanib Arfan (9)

Mourning Flowers

The bouquet of humanity has been ravaged
By the claws of evil;
We all stand aside in such awe as our silence
empowers the ignited flame,
Flame of envy and greed fuelled by innocence of mind.
Minds wired by the intelligence of need,
Needs to leave trees mourning for flowers buried six-foot underneath.
Underneath all the dirt and disease of conflict,
Conflict icing the cake of capitalism.
A cake that satisfies no hunger.

Samaya Heywood (16)

Changes

Summer, summer, ending soon,
The flowers have had their chance to bloom.
Leaves fall to the ground,
As autumn starts to show all around.

All the birds, now they know,
It's getting colder, time to go.
Hedgehogs burrow, ready to hibernate,
It's nearly autumn now, don't be late.

Another season has already passed,
Not long till Christmas now, at last!

Kalaya Partridge (10)

Squiffy - My Pet Cat

Squiffy is a cute little cat,
Sleeping on my bed
At night or day,
Even in the rain.

Squiffy likes my mother and my father,
Because they feed her every day.
She drinks from the pond - she once fell in!
And when she walks she plods all the way.

Squiffy is deaf so she doesn't miaow,
Instead she creaks like a rusty gate.
She's our cute little puffball,
With her furry back and her fluffy face.

We love our cat.

Eloise Fowle

Clayton's First Riddle

What could it be?
Follow the clues and see.

It looks **like blankies**.
It sounds **like talking**.
It smells **like dinner**.
It feels **happy**.
It tastes **like jelly**.

Have you guessed what it could be?
Look below and you will see,
It is...

Answer: My home.

Clayton Beaton (6)

My Best Friend

My best friend is so extremely kind
Because she helps me with anything on my mind

My best friend is the best at cheering me up
It is like she has some sort of magic touch

My best friend is like a sister to me
But I have to be careful because she is sometimes scary!

My best friend is sometimes very annoying,
But she never ever stops me from smiling.

Julia Hayek (10)

Summer!

I love summer!
Summer is hot,
It's sun and shade,
It's water to wade,
It's frogs and bugs,
It's grass for rugs,
It's tomato and corn.
It's eating outside,
It's a tree-swing ride,
It's family time,
And lots of noise.
It's a hot, sunny sky
It's summertime,
That's why
I love summer!

Karla Pipera (8)

Mother Nature

Nature is everywhere
Everywhere you see
Go down to the lake
None of the flowers are fake

Trees grow big and small
Nature is plants that grow so tall
Birds live in the trees
High in the sky or down low
Where the creatures live

So Mother Nature decides
Whether you should live or die
But there are thorns that can hurt you in the thigh.

Angel Wilkin (12)

Summer Of Dreams

On the perfect summer we...
Had some scoops of delicious ice cream
Lots of different flavours
Vanilla, mint choc-chip and cookies and cream
Having fun on beaches
Eating tropical fruit
Like peaches
We just made
Cool, fresh, scrumptious lemonade
Oh, all the competitions we won
The dream about summer on a tropical island
It was really fun!

Maya Dworak (10)

Be Amazed

The sky is a blanket of blue, white and sometimes black.
The sky is a room for you to relax.
The sky is a piece of paper, full of your imagination.
The sky is full of clouds shaped in your creation and is a mind vacation.
The sky is a bowl of all your thoughts swirled.
The sky is a boundary to all the secrets of the world.
So smile as you stand under the sky.

Sophia Currie (10)

The Happy Seasons

Twelve months in a row,
Use them well and let them go;
Welcome them without any fear,
Let them go without a tear.

Twelve months in a year,
Greet the passing miracles as they appear;
Spring and beautiful summer boarding on,
Then comes autumn and winter, gliding on;
Glorious seasons have quickly gone.

These are God's treasures in a row,
Take them, love them and let them go!

Gurmehr Grover (14)

Life

To save you from slander and infidelity
I am ready to blame myself
I don't understand the logic
You have wounded yourself to torment me
You are irreplaceable
Life is limited to express my feelings
You were saying I am a sinner, not a traitor
That was enough to believe
Without you I have no value
Your gaze was needed to make me priceless.

Zunairah Iqbal Raja (14)

Nature

Everything is nature
God gave us this feature
Let's see the birds that fly and sing
Let's see the green tree and see the clean water
Also see the four different seasons
Let's see the day and night
See the stars and moon
See the sun and see the high mountains
And then give thanks to the Lord
That he has given so many blessings.

Anoosha Fatima (14)

My Happy Place

As I go to the beach, holding a peach
I would see the warm sea gently coming to the sand
Also, I would see shells buried under the land
As I went down to the beach
Clutching my snack, a juicy peach
The warm sand beneath my feet
Had been warmed up with a wonderful heat
I could see shells from under the sand
This happy place is my special land.

Matilda Rhodes (9)

Róise's First Riddle

What could it be?
Follow the clues and see.

It looks **like a fluffy ball.**
It sounds **sniffy.**
It smells **nice like a teddy bear.**
It feels **really soft.**
It tastes **like carrots and dandelions.**

Have you guessed what it could be?
Look below and you will see,
It is...

Answer: A rabbit.

Róise McLernon (6)

Polly The Parrot

P olly Parrot on her tree
O ver the top of me
L ooking up
L ooking down
Y es, she flew away from me

P olly, Polly, please come back
A nd are you ready for a nap?
R est little Polly
R est and wake tomorrow
O pen up your eyes, Polly
T oday is tomorrow.

Ariyanna Turner-Rathbone (8)

A Day Of My Holiday

I was on my pirate ship, all was cool, ahoy my matey
The seagull flew fast at super speed, snooped in and stole the doughnut from my hand
I saw beautiful seashells in the deep blue sea
Riding on my enormous killer whale
Having a water fight with bursts of laughter
The sun coming down as the zzzs are coming out
Goodnight, see you tomorrow.

Ellis Mitchell (8)

Frustration Frenzy

I storm into my room
I slam the door
My ears fire and fume
I let out a mighty roar

I stomp my foot
It thumps the floor
It shakes and trembles the floor
I will have this no more

I slump into my bed
I am losing the plot
My face fiery red
My eyes are bloodshot

I let out one last roar
Shaking the ground and floor
I eventually close my eyes
My anger finally dies.

Callum Cayley (13)

The Monster Poem

Powers dark and powers bright,
I want you now as in my right,
Unleash the magic of this jewel,
And turn me into a monstrous fool

Tap it once, hair will show,
Tap it twice, legs will grow,
Tap it thrice, you will scream "Oh no!"

Powers high and powers low,
Change me back with one big blow,
I want my shape to return to me,
And become as I used to be.

Maysaa El Aoussi Hamdoun (11)

Things That Make Me Happy

T rampoline
H olidays
I ce cream
N umbers
G ames
S chool

T asty Brownies
H ome
A rt
T he caravan

M y family
A nimals
K inder eggs
E very dinosaur

M useums
E lectronics

H arry Potter
A nimal TV shows
P ets
P okémon
Y oghurts.

Austin Ford (7)

My Best Friend

They are your friend,
They are your pet,
They do have feelings,
So treat them the best.

You are their heart,
A cry of goodbye,
Treat them well,
Greet them hi,

You can have your laugh,
Have your cry,
They will always be by your side,

Show your pet love
And they will show it back!

Katie Thompson (13)

Desserts, Desserts, Desserts!

Desserts, desserts, desserts!
How I love cakes
And other delicious bakes!

Desserts, desserts, desserts!
I'm always alert when a dessert comes
Deserts deserve praise in all types of ways!

Desserts, desserts, desserts!
I'm crazy over desserts
When I eat too many, I get lazy!

Desserts, desserts, desserts!
I love desserts
Above everything else!

Maya Judge (11)

Baking A Cake

In my leisure, it's my pleasure...
I'll add all the ingredients to my bowl
I'll mix you and
I'll fiddle you all up
Till you're yummy enough for my tummy!

Though I'm satisfied, there's a lot to clean up
I'll brush you
I'll wash you
Till my kitchen is spick and span!

Amasha Ugathri Ganeshaparan (9)

My Small Little Hamster

My little hamster, small and round
Whenever he can, he runs around and around
In his ball, on his wheel
In his cage, he's a great big deal
He's slick and he's sly
But I wish he could fly
He's my little hamster, called Squid
In his ball, under my bed
That is where he would have hid.

Jorja Cleall (10)

The Weather

I like to look at the sky some days
As you can look at the clouds in many different ways
Every second changing in the sky so blue
As the weather is always new
That being rain or snow
It can be annoying when you have a place to go
It's nice to sit down and wonder
About what is happening far yonder.

James Worth (12)

I Am Nature

I can feel the wind in my hands.
I can feel the light in my heart
As the wind blows up the beaches sands.
Nature is a Pop-Tart.
Night and day are my every way
I can sing to the rain
Which makes it less insane.
I find nature in my soul
And the seas as they flow.
I know nature is amazing to me
And you can find it anywhere you see.

Vera Krauchuk-Muzhiv

The Fishy Day

One summer day,
Amazing day,
I had a big surprise!
I went for a walk
And took with me
My golden fishing rod,
It always brings me luck.
The sun was bright
The birds were joyful
Of the heat warming sun.
I found a brilliant place,
To try my luck.
An hour later I was going to give up.
Suddenly, in my surprise
I saw I caught
A fish!

Vadims Liss (9)

Strolling Through My Garden

Strolling through my garden
I think and contemplate

Strolling through my garden
Until it's very late

Strolling through my garden
I see the buzzing bees

Strolling through my garden
I play here when I please

Strolling through my garden
The roses dance and play

Strolling through my garden
This is where I choose to stay.

Erin Stedman (10)

Crystal Snowflake

Crystal ice snowflakes,
Falling,
Deep,
Deep,
Down
Its luminous light shining bright on the clear, tranquil river

As cold as an ice block
Its crystal look is charming
Icy-cold and shimmering in the diamond-white snow
Its charming love fits like a glove
Snow, snow, snow.

Savreen Kaur (10)

If I Had Wings

Inspired by 'If I Had Wings' by Pie Corbett

If I had wings
I would be like a hot-air balloon in the sky

If I had wings
I would lick the soft, fluffy clouds which taste like candyfloss

If I had wings
I would lay on the soft, smooth clouds

If I had wings
I would dream of walking the deserts and swimming the seas.

Agastya Dainak

Happy Birthday

My name is Zainab
I wanted to say happy 30th birthday
You are as sweet as a cute little unicorn
I wish you the brightest future and all that it can bring
May your every day be full of special things
Thank you for making us Young Writers
You are with us
We are with you
Happy birthday.

Zainab Channar (7)

Cool Clowns

C lowns always have red noses
O n time every time
O scar the Olympic clown
L ikes a ham and cheese sandwich

C rowds clapping and cheering
L aughs all around
O n top of elephants
W inning global awards
N ever ever gives up.

Charlie Barton (10)

Crazy Cats

Crazy, crazy cats galore,
Always knocking at my bedroom door.
In comes one, two, three then four,
Craving my attention, always wanting more.
Feeding time is like a zoo,
After eating they need the loo.
Then they have to take a nap,
Oh why, oh why do they always want to lay upon my lap?

Alana Marie Day (12)

Down The Dark Path

Walked down the dark path,
My hands shaking,
Heard a deep growl,
The monster was waking!
Lights were off,
A rumble in the floor,
Felt my heart beating,
I walked towards the door.
My heart beating triple speed,
Reached out my hand,
I opened the door,
"See Truth! I told you your puppy wasn't that bad!"

Truth Blunderfield (10)

Running

Running is fun for me
because of all the interesting things I see.
When I run in the blazing sun
something amazing happens to me!
In fluffy, white snow I run a bit slow,
Pouring rain makes me rush,
Through flashing, lightning strikes I dash
And not even the howling wind can stop me from running, running, running!

Zakariya Zaidi (8)

Me And My Mum

Me and my mum love to sit in the sun, guzzling cold 7-Up
We always work together, from now until forever
None of our meals are eaten without sharing each other's food
Even when we really aren't in the mood!
No matter what, we'll be besties forever
We stick together throughout all stormy weather.

Nafisa Khan (9)

My Birthday

B irthdays are a special day
I ncluding family and friends
R iddles and party games are fun to play
T he day is starting off great!
H aving delicious, yummy cake
D ay of fun and laughter
A new year with new adventures
Y ippee! It's my birthday today!

Nasif Khan (8)

I Like Someone

I like someone
That could be something
It could be me
Or be a bee
It lives on land
But it could be a plan
It could be he
But it's destined to be
It flies with thy
It has beautiful eyes
It's a parrot
Who knows, it could have been a carrot!

Simrat Kaur Gill Sandhu (10)

Birds

The first thing I remember is falling
I fell down and down out of my nest
Into the straw
A girl came up to me
She fed me and looked after me
In a few weeks I was better
So I was put in a cage
And soon a week was gone
She opened my cage
She smiled
And I flew away
For I am a bird and birds fly free.

Siân Watson (7)

The Possibilities Of My Future

My future is ahead of me
I am thinking of my possibilities
I believe that I am eager to write
I believe I know wrong from right
I want to make my mark
Before my life goes dark
I must try to write more poetry
So I can show people the real me
I can see my possibilities
How can it become a reality?

Arghojit Giri (16)

The Lie

The lie,
What lie?
The lie,
The lie of the world,
The largest most drastic lie,
The lie of lies,
The queen of lies
The lie surrounding humanity,
We 'rulers of the Earth',
Are not so.
There is a higher power,
The highest power,
The mother of all things,
And her name,
Is Mother Nature.

Amy Holding (12)

It Only Needs One Line

I just want reassurance
Everyone wants that,
I want to go home
Everyone wants that,

I just want a hug
Everyone wants that,
I just want fame
Everyone wants that,

I just want money
Everyone wants that,
I just want to be happy
That's not what everyone wants,
It's what everyone needs.

Emily Rudd (14)

Magical Unicorn

Unicorn, unicorn sleep sweet and sound
May all your dreams be found
Unicorn, unicorn I love you
Unicorn, unicorn I need you
Unicorn, unicorn pink and blue
Please make all my wishes come true
Unicorn, unicorn I said goodbye
Maybe I'll see you next time!

Ellen Durham (8)

Wind Haiku And Cinquain

Haiku

The wind which blows me
Magical moment begins
I whizz through the sky.

Cinquain

Wind, wind
You are my friend
You race along with me
Here and there, everywhere, tick-tock
Whizz! Pop!

Shifa Fatima (8)

The Bright Night

Night-night, sleep tight
Don't let the bed bugs bite
Or the constellation in the night
Otherwise they will give you a fright
And then you'll have to turn on the lights
But then it will be too bright
And you won't be able to sleep tonight.

Elizabeth Holmes (8)

Happy 30th Birthday

A is for age
B is for birthday
C is for cake, come have some
D is for dancing, swing those hips
E is for everyone, join in the fun
F is for friends and family
G is for gifts
H is for... Happy 30th birthday to the Young Writers' team!

Leigha Mcgarva (10)

Lion

L azy lion lying on the ground on a hot summer's day
I ncredible lion creeps quietly, closer towards his prey
O ld lion licks what is left of an antelope bone
N oisily, the male lion roars to show who's the boss to the cubs.

Briannika Rae Brown (8)

What Is Gold?

Gold looks like a buttercup, bright and shiny and light.
Gold sounds like rustling leaves, over the mountain tops high and low.
Gold smells like ten thousand rich pound coins.
Gold tastes like caramel.
Gold feels hard like steel.
It reminds me of stars beyond our reach.

George Frank Gamble (7)

My Unicorn Friend

Once I met a unicorn
And I found out she was magic
Up on the clouds
She lived with her friends
She was cotton candy-pink
And had feathery wings
Her colourful hair
Swayed with care
And Sugar was her name
My unicorn friend.

Lana Khoshnaw (6)

The Beach

Crystal waves roll in
Froth dissolves into the sand
The horizon reaches far in sight
Gregarious birds glide with pride
Balls of cotton litter the sky
Shades of the sunset soothe in
Golden grit blanket the ground
The lenient breeze whistles smoothly
This is my home.

Elsa Hussain (13)

Fantastic Football

I love football, it's the best!
I love to play, I'm so obsessed.
When I score I scream and shout!
I love football without a doubt.
When I'm older I'd like to play for a team,
Become a pro and accomplish my dream.

Archie Embleton

Super Penguin

Super penguin flies around
She whizzes and fizzes
Her name is Sparkle
She can go quick in the sky and in the deep blue sea,
Waddle, waddle! Taddle, taddle!
She holds an ice blaster and throws it around
She is the best pet ever in the universe.

Syeda-Zahra Iftikhar (6)

How Much I Love My Panda

Panda, kanda, sanda... whatever
I love my panda no matter what he's called
I love him in a tree
I love him in the sea
I even love him riding on a bee
But most of all I love him hugging me
Panda is my favourite teddy.

Libbie Reid (9)

Spring Is Here!

Spring has come! Spring is here!
Birds cheerfully chirping on the trees.
Leaves dancing happily with the breeze.
Fluffy flowers blossoming magnificently.
Busy bees buzzing noisily.
Bouncy bunnies hopping happily.
Spring is fun! Spring is the best!

Nusayba Ahmed (9)

My Teddy Bear

I have a teddy bear,
that can do the scary stare.

He might remind you of a hare,
but he's a bear, I swear.

I like to dress him up every day,
with clothes in every way.

Oh, my little teddy bear,
you'll always be in my care.

Gabriela Sosnowska (12)

Be Yourself!

The Earth we see is where people live
In our world we see the past behind us
We shall care for our schools, our parents and families
Enjoy the sunshine in the day
And those fears are hours away
Be yourself!

Madeleine Sibley (8)

My Football Dream

Hear the crowd roar
When England score

Hear the crowd roar
When Ipswich score

Hear the crowd roar
When Stewart scores

Hear the crowd cheer
Because Stewart is here.

Logan Stewart (7)

I Like Owls

I like owls,
Because they have big eyes,
They peer into the night
And find dirty rats,
They find food
That is very yummy
So, do you like owls now
Because they are my favourite?

Sophia Tang (7)

I Am Special

I am special.
I have 16 centimetres of light blond hair.

I am special.
I love leaves and trees and the missing cat.

I am special.
I like how the sun gives life to the whole planet.

Fred Gamble (6)

Pinky The Cane

Pinky the cane
Helps me to see
Going to school
And back again
It's so much fun
With Pinky the cane
Going tab, tab, tab
And roll, roll, roll.

Evia Shaw-Lewis (8)

My Fluffy Puppy!

I have a dog,
I love her very much.
She has fluffy ears and cute black eyes.
I like her nose and her little mouth.
I cuddle her and play all days,
She makes me very happy.

Katrina Lise (6)

Tigers

T igers are talented
I n the wild forest
G rowling super loudly
E xtremely wild and scary
R oaring all the time.

Nahida Forid (7)

Fly Away

It flies away in the distance
As the wind howls away
And is unlikely to come back again
As I wake up I wonder, *will I ever see it again?*

Maham Muhammad (12)

Poor Sid

There once was a snail called Sid
Who slipped and slimed and slid
He slipped on ice
Which wasn't very nice
And banged his head did Sid.

Bella-May Conway (8)

Lockdown

Lockdown, lock up,
Going in the garden, I've had enough.
Home learning, it sucks!
But no school, things are looking up...

Charlie Carroll (11)

Nature's Beauty

As I walk into the wood what do I see?
I see deer leaping
Birds gliding
Bunnies hopping
And bright colourful flowers.

Oluwasemilore Isabelle Abiola

Gems

Diamonds are see-through
But our sadness is too
Rubies are red
And anger is in bed.

Yumi Smith (8)

Young Writers Information

We hope you have enjoyed reading this book – and that you will continue to in the coming years.

If you're the parent or family member of an enthusiastic poet or story writer, do visit our website **www.youngwriters.co.uk/subscribe** and sign up to receive news, competitions, writing challenges and tips, activities and much, much more! There's lots to keep budding writers motivated!

If you would like to order further copies of this book, or any of our other titles, then please give us a call or order via your online account.

Young Writers
Remus House
Coltsfoot Drive
Peterborough
PE2 9BF
(01733) 890066
info@youngwriters.co.uk

Join in the conversation!
Tips, news, giveaways and much more!

YoungWritersUK   YoungWritersCW   youngwriterscw